Literacy Activities for Building Classroom Communities

ARDITH DAVIS COLE

Pippin Publishing

212751

Copyright © 1998 by Pippin Publishing Corporation
Suite 232
85 Ellesmere Road
Scarborough, Ontario
M1R 4B9

Edited by Anne Fullerton
Designed by John Zehethofer
Typeset by Jay Tee Graphics Ltd.
Printed and bound in Canada by Friesens

Canadian Cataloguing in Publication Data

Cole, Ardith Davis
    Literacy activities for building classroom activities

(The Pippin teacher's library)
Includes bibliographical references.
ISBN 0-88751-078-7

1. Reading (Elementary). 2. English language – Study and teaching (Primary). I. Title. II. Series.

LB1525.C65   372.4   C97-931485-2

ISBN 0-88751-078-7

10   9   8   7   6   5   4   3   2   1

This book is dedicated to
ROBERT M. WILSON,
who started me on the journey into
reading and its instruction
and
in loving memory of
ANTOINETTE BERENT,
who supported me as a I continued that journey
down the glorious but sometimes bumpy road
to a new paradigm.

ACKNOWLEDGEMENTS

During this work's 12-year evolution, numerous individuals helped shape its contents. But most of the thoughts that danced their way into the reality of this text were carved by the children in my classrooms at Charlotte Cross Elementary School in Lockport, New York. Their happy faces shine through both the words and the pictures.

I will always appreciate the thoughtful assistance I received from Pippin Publishing, from Jonathan Lovat Dickson, who so caringly nurtured the entire process, and from my editor, Anne Fullerton, whose kind and knowledgeable guidance make her a very special person. I learned so much from Anne. I also want to thank several of my colleagues, who read and responded to the early drafts of this work — Dr. Elaine Garan of Eastern New Mexico University, Dr. Maria Ceprano of St. Bonaventure University, Linda Schott, the teacher with whom I worked at Charlotte Cross Elementary School, and Dr. Michelle Kavanaugh, the principal of Maplemere, where I now work. Of course, my family, friends and colleagues have been a great support throughout.

C O N T E N T S

INTRODUCTION

> In the night he changed from following the deer to
> becoming the deer. A part of him went out to the deer and
> a part of the deer went out of her into him, across the white
> light and he wasn't the same. He would never be the same
> again. He was of the deer and the snow and the night and
> he kept himself but he lost his spirit and gained a new one.
>
> Gary Paulsen, *Tracker*

I was for a very long time a ditto queen. I thought that dittos helped control the class, that they ensured all students were in their seats "doing their own work." I thought that dittos taught children, that they monitored them as they progressed through an increasingly difficult curriculum, making certain that all skills were "covered." That was why my students did so well on standardized tests. Or so I thought.

I believed that I needed dittos to teach each and every skill—every short *a*, every long *e*, every schwa, blend, and diphthong. How else would my students learn sequencing, main idea, and "best titles?" Dittos laid the foundation for reading. Or so I thought.

I also thought substitute teachers wouldn't know what to do with the kids unless I left a tall stack of dittos. I even stockpiled stacks in case a sub ran out of the variety that covered my desk. Not that this variety indicated a choice, for substitutes had no choice. No, I had very explicit plans that drove the curriculum and all human beings who traversed the grounds of *my* classroom.

During those years, I could proudly proclaim that I was in control, and my yearly performance evaluation confirmed my success. But in my heart I knew that I shared the key to that success with the daily dittos, for without those fill-in-the-blank shackles that bound children to their desks, my control kingdom might indeed crumble. Or so I thought.

While I admit that my students were deluged with dittos, think not that I spent my evenings searching through sources to copy. As a matter of fact, I never purchased any of those blackline masters that companies sell under such misnomers as "Comprehension Skills Practice" or "Main Idea Exercises." I didn't even use the blackline masters that accompanied the district basals. I often said, "It takes teachers longer to copy these masters than it does for the kids to do them." A definite waste of time as far as I was concerned. Instead, I created my own dittos, most of which contained open-ended questions. For instance, to provide vocabulary practice, I made pages of stem sentences whose endings could be constructed by the children. The sentences might go something like this: "My mom and I like to go _____." Or I'd put sentences in boxes, leaving room for students to draw accompanying pictures. I felt especially confident with my carefully con-structed comprehension questions, which I based on "higher levels of thinking." After each and every story, I called the students to their reading groups so that we could go over their answers together—meaning that students would read their responses and then revise those that were "wrong." I felt I was doing everything that behaviorist theory espoused. The students and I went over their work right after they finished it. Each student corrected his own work, coming away with the "right" answer to all questions. Every paper went home with the reward of a smiling face at the top. I knew how to teach reading. Or so I thought.

My students' parents celebrated all the wonderful "work" their children did, as well as the fact that it was completed before it was brought home. And with their adorned refrig-erators and walls standing as testimony to their children's successes, the parents shared their pride with others and with me, further validating my success.

But in fact, it was a parent who sowed the first seeds of my seatwork discontent. One June, Steven's father, a minister, announced from the pulpit that among his family's recent accomplishments were the 1200 dittos and workbook pages his son had done in Mrs. Cole's classroom. That little com-ment provoked a series of questions. I wondered if Steven's father thought that his son, who was in my "top group," was a good worker and was celebrating his achievements. But I also wondered if the minister's comments might have contained a note of sarcasm, that he was suggesting how silly our educational practices can sometimes be. I wondered if he resented all the work his little six-year-old had had to do. Perhaps he thought that curious, energetic six-year-olds should be doing activities other than filling in the blanks on 1200 dittos.

That was 1966. Unfortunately, it was many more years before the seedlings of my discontent took root, and more still before their new form burst through layers of curriculum, social structures, and politics and out into the light of common sense. It was a very long time before I questioned the whole use of seatwork. Certainly not all of it needed to be questioned.... Or did it?

I had always tried not to neglect creativity completely, and thus not all of the seatwork I assigned belonged to the Kingdom of Right and Wrong Answers. For instance, sometimes children were invited to write a "little story" related to a given topic or title. I remember celebrating their creations with the class and saving many until year's end, when I published them in booklets called *First Grade Writing* or *Third Grade Stories*. Other "exercises" with no single right answer required students to arrange letters into words or words into sentences. "Let's see who can build the most sentences," I'd call out. "The winner will get a prize!" Not bad for 1967. Or so I thought.

At that time I didn't think kids would "work" very hard unless I offered an enticing reward. There was also always an incentive to "get your work done so that you can have free time." During "free" time children could read a book to themselves (quietly), paint at the easel (quietly), draw a picture (quietly), or use the clay (quietly). As each year grew to look much like the previous one, my own creative soul began to nurture those seeds planted in a minister's sermon. A variety of whole group activities gradually enlivened the humdrum of our classroom world. Together, my students and I enjoyed grandparents' tea parties, plays, walks, elaborate art projects, and activities that incorporated the language experience approach. As we deviated from the fill-in-the-blank curriculum, I became aware of something special growing within our classroom. It was many years before I could define that "something special." In the mid-1980s I attended a week-long conference conducted by a number of New Zealand teachers. As I watched videos taken in their classrooms, I became aware that that same "something special" was occurring there. I gathered everything I could from those visiting teachers and went back to my own classroom committed to constructing this different kind of environment, a community in which children smiled more, talked more, shared more, and cared more.

Youngsters the world over grow up amidst verbal interaction, learning to work and play in talk-filled environments. They do, that is, until they move into a new culture, an often different world of quiet and control: the classroom. But when we gaze upon the old institutional settings of the schoolroom with new eyes, we begin to realize how important it is to change those century-old classroom climates and replace them with exciting, active environments, where talk is not only encouraged but also celebrated.

To start such a change in my own classroom, I had to move away from models structured on independent reading and writing and replace the activities that focused on filling in the blanks. With my new way of seeing, I began to realize that if students knew the answer, they were not learning anything or creating, but merely regurgitating in an attempt to give me what I wanted. I began to realize that learners had not been constructing their *own* personal meanings in my classroom, and that most seatwork activities were therefore nothing more than testing situations. According to researchers Dolores Durkin and Rebecca Barr, who studied how teachers teach, I was definitely among the majority in my seatwork mentality—a treadmill difficult to abandon.

At first I found it intimidating to move into settings where students worked together most of the day. It seemed likely that while I worked with one group, others, no longer chained to their dittos, might get out of control. In fact, Elaine Garan, a researcher who visited my classroom in the early '90s, wrote that "the greatest revelation of this study was the realization of how deep the need to control is within those of us in education...the temptation to remain in control is formidable." She saw that I had to "struggle continually and recommit to taking risks in order to live [my] beliefs. Allowing children to assume responsibility both for classroom management and for their own learning was not neat and orderly, nor was it a linear process. [I] had to risk the threat of children off task, noise (both productive and non-productive), and the 'silent voids' that beckoned to [me], begging to be filled with teacher-directed comments and questions."

In hindsight, this seems somewhat ironic, for I have come to understand that "controlling the students" was not even the issue. The real issue is not so much whether the students might be out of control, but rather who should have control in the first place. Should the teacher be controlling the students, or should the students be controlling themselves? I think most of us would answer that ultimately students must control their own behaviors.

I came to discover that when the focus of a classroom is community, where students work and support one another, "getting out of control" is not usually an issue. As a matter of fact, I found that most often youngsters within such an environment become so involved with their community's activities that they must eventually be coaxed to stop. They often develop a passion for the activity, as well as for the discipline of study. In such an environment students claim the kind of ownership of learning that creates a commitment to it. This work is a mixture of the theory and practice of a model for teaching reading that finds its real essence within a caring and sharing community. The first part of the book describes the foundation of both the model and the community. In the second part, this model is demonstrated through the use of vignettes set within a variety of communities. The names of the characters in these vignettes are those of colleagues, and pieces and parts of the stories might have been captured within any of their classrooms, although no one story could be said to have actually happened. Likewise, most of these little stories could have happened within my own classroom communities; but again, with the exception of one autobiographical vignette, none of the accounts evolved exactly as portrayed.

I have known the mechanics of teaching reading for a very long time, but until I came to understand the relevance of community, the process lacked the spirit needed to create a more caring classroom world. When I changed, the children began learning through social experiences that taught them how to care for and about not only subject matter but also one another. Within such a community, all learning is a journey toward success!

PREREADING

Develop Enthusiasm
Review Vocabulary Quickly
Visualization Paints the Picture
Develop Story Scheme
Strategies Aid the Process

THE READING ACT

DEPENDENT APPROACHES

Teacher Read-Alouds
Taped Recordings
Computer Programmed Stories and Videos

SEMI-DEPENDENT APPROACHES

Paired Reading
The Shared Book Experience
Guided Reading Approaches

INDEPENDENT APPROACHES

Schema-Base
Extended Reading
Sustained Silent Reading
Recreational Reading

POSTREADING

Sharing
Discussion and Conversation
Research

. . . .

BRINGING CHILDREN TO
STORY: A SUPPORT MODEL

Teachers need to set up their classrooms so that children
rely on their own personal and social resources rather than
solely on the teacher. When they use their own support
networks, children develop cooperative social patterns that
are likely to be functional outside school.

Jerome Harste, Kathy Short, and Carolyn Burke

Bringing children to story is at the heart of literacy
and has probably been in the hearts of many wonderful teachers since reading and writing began. In fact, researchers such
as Jerome Bruner, Arthur Applebee, and Michael Halliday tell
us that story is actually the basis of language.

There are a variety of ways in which we can bring children
to story. Just as parents support children in their early attempts at language, so too can teachers support children in
their early attempts at reading. However, the level and quantity of this help depends on the child and the text. It is the
responsibility of the teacher to discover avenues of support
for learners in their search for story. This changing role of
the teacher—from that of "filler of empty vessels" to that of
a facilitator, mediator, or coach—gives impetus to the revi-
sion of old models of teaching. The following presents such
a revised model, through which literacy activities can gain
meaning. The model is structured around three sometimes
overlapping segments of prereading, the reading act, and
postreading.

Prereading

In the new model, prereading, traditionally the skill-and-
drill part of the lesson, is now a time to support and enthuse
the learner. One might make an analogy here to what an

adult does to interest a fellow adult in a piece of literature. For instance, if I read a good book, I usually give one (or more) of my friends a copy. It is also common for me to share favorite parts of the story, even reading excerpts over the phone. It only makes sense that we, as teachers, should incorporate into our classrooms some of the tactics we use in our private lives. We do not term our enticing friends and family to read books we have read "prereading," but that's certainly what it is. We know that if we do a good enough job with these enticements, those whom we lure will indeed read what we've recommended, for there is something about story that captivates us.

In the classroom, such enticement also makes the reading process more predictable for learners. That is, if students know what to expect from their eventual reading experience, they will tend to view the act of reading as increasingly accessible. But beginning readers need other kinds of pre-reading support. We all know that the nature of support differs from one text to another and from one student to the next. Several qualifiers help teachers sense the amount of support needed: (1) the number of times the student has read this or similar texts; (2) the qualities (difficulty of words, content, etc.) inherent in each text; and (3) the background information needed to tread these particular textual pathways. Some texts provide structural support patterns, such as rhyme and repetition. Many also fit into a predictable genre—that is, the general literary pattern that makes a fairy tale a fairy tale, a riddle a riddle, or a letter a letter. (For example, most of us can predict at least some of the elements that will appear in a text beginning "Once upon a time....") Although some texts may have schemes familiar to most students, others may be very foreign. Some texts may have common, high-frequency vocabulary; others may have challenging or even strange words. Even highly literate adults need help moving comfortably through certain texts. (I, myself, needed support during a recent journey through a book describing fractals.) Careful selection of texts will facilitate all prereading activities and ensure that students are engaged as they approach the reading act.

What type of activities can help students attain the benefits of prereading? How can we provide the right kind of support? This can be done in many ways.

DEVELOP ENTHUSIASM

How many times have you read half of a poignant magazine article to a friend, spouse, son, or daughter, anticipating that they will follow and read the remainder? How many times have you purchased a book because a friend or relative said, "Oh, you have to read..." and then went on to tell you half the story? Enthusiasm is contagious. The more impassioned we are, the more enthused our students will be. Likewise, the more excited children are about a piece of literature, the more confident they feel about approaching the reading act. This places considerable responsibility on us, for our students sense whether we are actively involved with literature; they interpret us through our behaviors as much as through our words. We need to take stock of our demonstrations. Are we exhibiting a love of story? For it is the love of story that will stimulate.

REVIEW VOCABULARY QUICKLY

Although students may know the meaning of a word and use it frequently in oral language, they may still have trouble decoding it in its printed form. This is common at the beginning of the literacy journey. Such frequently occurring but difficult-to-decode words are usually called "sight vocabulary." Nouns, with their concrete meanings, are often easy to learn, but novice readers may require several exposures to words such as "who," "saw," and "once" before they are committed to long-term memory. So, although beginning readers may initially have difficulty decoding easy texts with few words, the meanings of these words are not usually a problem. Yet all readers, novice and skilled alike, occasionally come across a word whose meaning may be in question. We might term these unknowns "meaning vocabulary." That is, a word such as "ilk" can be easily decoded by many beginning readers but may not be understood without the prereading support of a teacher.

We should keep in mind, however, that although it is helpful to introduce difficult vocabulary before reading, researchers Michael Kibby, Harry Singer, and Marshall Arlin and colleagues all found that the time spent on this should be minimal. Knowledge of vocabulary is solidified in the context of story. That is, a brief introduction of either sight or meaning vocabulary will suffice, for as a student encounters these words within text, they will gradually find their way into the mind's storehouse.

VISUALIZATION PAINTS THE PICTURE

With the onslaught of images found in music videos, movies, and video games, youngsters now rely less and less on the pictures created by their minds' eyes. The seemingly near-extinct ability to create mental images needs to find its way into prereading lessons so that, as the setting and characters of the upcoming story are discussed, students can paint pictures of them on the canvasses of their minds. This, in turn, will provide nourishment for the roots of story. Having students simply close their eyes and "picture" can work wonders, for it can serve as a strategy for the meaning-making that occurs later during reading. When students have images in their minds' eyes, they seem better equipped and more eager to find out how those images give form to meaning. Also, Laura Rose, basing her assertion on brain research, suggests that "every time a child sees the whole picture (right brain) and puts a verbal or symbolic label on it (left brain), the communication track between the two brain hemispheres is utilized and thereby strengthened."

DEVELOP STORY SCHEME

Often a discussion of how a story "works" can provide a good step into reading. The teacher can, of course, prompt a discussion by talking about elements of a story's scheme. Sometimes, however, it is not the teacher who invites, but other students. In such prereading activities, students can share their own links with a story's setting, theme, characters, feelings, and other aspects. This will lay personal foundations for reading.

Story schemes can also be developed through reading related texts or works by the same author, providing graphic organizers, and storytelling. Reading other works by the same author or related to the same topic can provide a "scaffold," so that as students enter the act of reading a new text an air of familiarity will support their journey. For instance, before students begin reading the works of Robert Munsch, I might read aloud *Thomas's Snowsuit*, one of my favorites. I would follow this with an invitation to listen to an audiotape of Munsch telling some of his fantastic tales. With this sort of foundation, how can students do anything but succeed as they make the journey through a Munsch text themselves?

With more mature readers, I often read aloud a chapter or two of the selected text to lay a similar kind of foundation. This taste of the whole also tantalizes potential readers. Besides introducing characters and setting, such prereading steeps listeners in the author's voice and the text style. It is frequently this particular lure that entices the reader further into the text.

Another prereading activity for developing story scheme involves the use of graphic organizers. These provide a different kind of cognitive structure for stories as they depict hierarchically organized elements or closely related topics or events in graphic form. Such an organizer can be presented prior to the reading of the story so that as students read, they

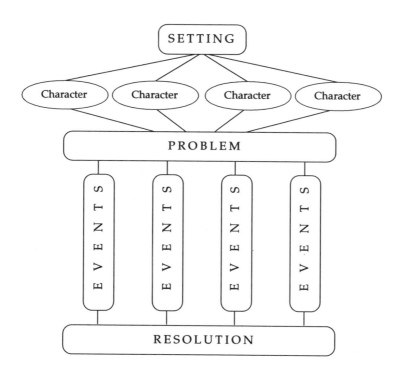

A prototype graphic organizer illustrating story structure

can reference pieces of this connected information to help in their own meaning-making.

Sometimes teachers also use storytelling or drama as a prereading aid to develop story background. Teachers can encourage this by modeling storytelling and then providing opportunities for students to collect and share well-known stories. After all, stories began in our culture as oral events, not as written texts. As a matter of fact, the interpretation of ancient myths, legends, and parables in films and videos can provide yet another foundational element for the development of story background in the reader.

STRATEGIES AID THE PROCESS

During prereading, it is beneficial to frequently review strategies that allow for optimal decoding of text. This is especially important for students who tend to rely on the teacher or others. We must help children understand that readers access three cue systems—semantics (meaning), syntax (sentence grammar), and graphophonemics (sound-symbol relationships)—and make them aware of strategies founded on each so that they can move along the road to independence in reading.

In the area of semantics, readers need to be encouraged to reread for meaning when something is unclear or seems not to make sense. They also need to use the illustrations for support. But sometimes they need to just skip over or "muddle through" the unknown or confusing words and then reread after they have collected the meaning vested in the rest of the sentence. In this way, readers can make reasonable guesses at the meanings of unfamiliar words.

Above all, readers must know that the sentence should make sense. If it doesn't, a metaphoric red light should signal in the reader the need for a self-correction strategy.

Readers who guess at an unfamiliar word should also be reminded that any substitute must keep with the grammatical flow—the syntax—of the sentence, that is, it must be the same part of speech. If, for example, a student is unsure of the meaning of "prowl" when it is presented in isolation, she might recognize it as the action of a burglar in the sentence "The burglar prowled around the empty house."

As readers employ meaning and grammar strategies, they need simultaneously to check whether the sound-symbol relationship of what is being read is congruent. For instance, the reader who reads "We all listened to the barking of the dogs" may feel secure that what he read made sense and was grammatically sound. Yet this reader did not attend closely to the graphics, because in the text the sentence actually was "We all listened to the barking of the seals." Such a reader would then be encouraged to focus carefully on sound-symbol relationships. At other times, however, semantics or syntax must be the focus. A reader who does not self-correct when she reads, "The gril brushed her teeth," is not reading for meaning but is relying on sound-symbol relationships. Obviously, grills do not have teeth to brush!

It is evident that all cue systems must work in harmony, and that good readers use a variety of strategies to decode in a meaningful manner. During prereading activities it is useful to conduct minilessons on strategies that focus on all three cue systems. Yetta Goodman, Dorothy Watson, and Carolyn Burke's *Reading Miscue Inventory* is an excellent resource on strategy use, as is Don Holdaway's *The Foundations of Literacy*. For those students who continue to rely on the teacher and others to get through the text, it might be wise to respond to their pleas with "What strategies have you used to try to do it yourself?"

SUMMARY

It is important to provide the necessary support for the reading act, even though this support will differ from child to child and text to text. Teachers can develop a repertoire of support activities that will provide a scaffold for even the most tentative learner or the most challenging text. Sometimes this may mean actually reading the story to the learner. It is then that the new reading model's recursive nature becomes apparent: the prereading activity actually becomes part of the second stage, or "the reading act."

The Reading Act

Educators are now taking a broader view of the reading act. The traditional classroom model, which permeates pre-1990s basal manuals, was generally founded on Anthony Manzo's guided reading procedure, Emmett Betts's Directed Reading Activity, or Russell Stauffer's Directed Reading-Thinking Activity. Such approaches have in common a fairly formal structure and emphasize initial silent reading of text. However, current research suggests a variety of other ways to approach story in the classroom. Along with this research has come a focus on the quality of the reading or of the story experience itself.

In today's classrooms, teachers can often be seen using techniques that vary from very supportive (when the student is completely dependent on the teacher or another more proficient reader) to minimally supportive (when the reader can process print independently). Obviously the amount of support required is determined by the text as well as by the child. And although our goal is to help readers become independent, there will always be times when support is needed—even for adults.

The following section provides examples of techniques offering support at each of three levels:

— dependent approaches (for the most dependent emergent reader)
— semi-dependent approaches (for the blossoming or insecure reader)
— independent approaches (for the independent reader).

DEPENDENT APPROACHES

Sometimes we need to invite youngsters to let us be the entertainers as they sit back and simply enjoy story and the experiences in language that we can model. The best predictor of children's reading success in school is the amount of reading aloud they experienced as preschoolers. The benefits of reading aloud can certainly be extended into the classroom. Furthermore, teachers often discover that the books students are apt to read themselves are those that have been read aloud to them. Reading aloud is obviously a way of sharing the reading act with dependent readers. But a read-aloud situation can also serve as a prereading demonstration of what more advanced readers do as they read. That is, the teacher-reader can stop periodically, inviting the audience to predict what might happen next in the story or simply to make a comment to a neighbor. Teachers can also make connections to other pieces of literature or encourage listeners to reflect on the way story relates to their own lives.

Read-alouds contain many other subtle yet important demonstrations. They show listeners how skilled readers use inflection, intonation, eye contact, and timing. The audience learns "read-aloud etiquette," which includes how to show the pictures and how to invite audience participation. Also, through such experiences teachers model the language of story, which helps listeners become more confident to take risks. Indeed, read-alouds provide a safe, warm world for story.

Taped recordings of stories provide a different type of read-aloud experience and offer more support than is found within a directed reading lesson. Through taped recordings emergent readers can receive the imprint of the language of text—that is, the melody of text, as well as its schemes, becomes a part of their memory store, making subsequent encounters with printed stories more predictable. With taped recordings, children generally follow along with their own copy of the text, listening to the entire story or portions of it as often as they like. These are the "repeated readings" advocated by S. Jay Samuels. For those who are learning to read they often provide the needed support to carry a youngster into fluency. As a novice journeys through the same story again and again, pointing to the printed words while listening to a taped recording, he is learning many things about the reading experience. Indeed, for novice readers to gain enough confidence and ability to actually decode independently, they must have many, many opportunities to follow along as a story is read aloud to them. This following along or "fingerpointing" activity may be *the* most important experience a teacher can provide for the novice. Perhaps this is why the chant "Point, point, point to the words" rings through the corridors that house kindergarten and primary classrooms.

These read-aloud techniques can be performed by all teachers, but modern technology continues to provide us with new ways to approach instruction and support learning. For those with access to them, computer programs offering stories whose words are highlighted as they are read orally can support dependent readers as they move toward fluency. With such programs the student is in control: she can direct the program to repeat words, make pictures come to life, and so on. Videotapes of stories with "subtitles" of the words being read are also available. Some videos go one step further in enticing the viewer into the act by adopting a "karaoke" approach: children are invited to read-sing their way through the tape while the highlighted text stays right in step with the music!

SEMI-DEPENDENT APPROACHES

As developing readers begin to gain more confidence they find that the need for support gradually decreases, although the amount required will always be related to the nature of the text. Responding accordingly, the observant teacher uses techniques that provide support in varying degrees. Two popular techniques that pair more competent readers with the novice have their roots in Heckelman's neurological impress remedial technique of the 1960s. With this method, the teacher or another proficient reader reads aloud, while pointing at the words. The student joins in the oral reading, following the teacher's lead. At first the proficient reader reads loudly, but gradually the student begins to take over until fluency is reached. In the 1980s Keith Topping began studying the positive effects of what he called "paired reading," and Patricia Koskinen and Irene Blum contrasted this with their "peer tutoring." In these approaches the teacher or another partner encourages the learner to read until she experiences difficulty. At that point the partner subtly takes over until the learner chimes in confidently enough to move along independently again, as though they were waltzing through the text together. Although time-consuming, this kind of one-on-one instruction can be used within a classroom, for with very little modeling by the teacher, independent, confident readers in the class can act as partners for others who might be experiencing difficulty. These peer tutoring situations have proven to be very effective. Also, with a brief explanation and a modeling session, parents of emergent readers can provide yet another avenue for this kind of support.

The Shared Book Experience, brought into prominence by Don Holdaway in his *The Foundations of Literacy*, provides another type of support. In this whole-to-parts approach, the teacher models the reading of a predictable story. Often she reads from an enlarged text, such as a big book, to enable group viewing. After the initial reading, the children are invited to join in. Stronger readers then vocally support weaker ones. After repeated readings the students can read the big book (or a smaller version) with a partner or independently. And emergent readers should be encouraged to point to the words during these rereadings. This helps move the novice from memorizing to actually attending closely to the words.

After a number of rereadings (over a few days, perhaps), the teacher returns to the book for a different purpose. Now that the text is very familiar, she uses it to teach reading skills within the context of the story. She might mask some words, encouraging readers to guess what's missing, or she might ask students to find words that end in "-ing" or "-ed." Any number of other skills and strategies can be taught in this manner.

Sometimes, when confronted by more difficult text, even competent readers need the support of shared reading. Often poetry, expository works, or the classics (children's versions of Shakespeare, for example) call for this approach. Roger Farr uses a technique he calls "Read-Alongs," which is very similar to Richard Allington's "Think-Along." In such methods, printed matter is enlarged through the use of a transparency to help readers focus on particular connections, strategies, writing techniques, or elements of a certain genre. By thinking aloud about such aspects of text, the teacher demonstrates how mature readers process the printed word—that is, they predict, make connections, wonder, question, validate, and so on. Many of us might have enjoyed the works of Shakespeare or texts such as *Silas Marner* in high school or college had our teachers introduced these difficult classics using a read-along or Shared Book Experience.

Guided reading approaches such as the Directed Reading Activity and the Directed Reading-Thinking Activity offer another avenue for providing support for developing readers. In such approaches, the teacher "guides" the students through the text in one manner or another. Although guided or directed reading was a part of the old basal instruction, it is still a very valid technique for use in classroom communities founded on new literacy approaches. The Directed Reading Activity (or DRA), a basic building block of the '70s and '80s basal instruction, incorporates a sequence of activities. First, the teacher prepares the students by establishing a purpose for reading, introducing vocabulary, and setting the background. Then the students read the text silently, after which it is discussed through teacher-generated questions (this segment is usually called Comprehension). Next comes oral or silent rereading (again called Comprehension), and finally, the teacher focuses on skills, generally in isolation and out of story context, along with occasional enrichment activities. The Directed Reading-Thinking Activity (or DRTA) has a similar structure but focuses on predication and verification. In the prereading portion of the activity, students predict what they will read, verifying and then validating those predictions during reading and postreading.

These approaches take on a different form in today's classrooms, where skills are taught in context and where activities do not center around workbooks and ditto sheets. Furthermore, postreading conversations now allow for exploration of text by students, and the reading experience is not undertaken to measure children's ability but to nurture experiences that help create lifelong readers.

A guided approach and the Shared Book Experience are sometimes confused. The basic but important difference between the two is that the former offers somewhat less support, in that the text is not first read aloud (modeled) for the students. Instead, each child is expected to read the text independently after the teacher and the students have completed supportive prereading activities. These prereading activities are expected to activate the readers' cue systems (that is, semantics, syntax, and graphophonemics), thereby enabling her to progress independently and strategically through the text. Less fluent readers who need more support can obtain it through incorporation of a more dependent approach, such as the Shared Book Experience.

INDEPENDENT APPROACHES

The final goal of all reading instruction, independence, places the responsibility completely on the learner. When that goal is reached, the student knows what he is able to read and can access the necessary strategies to process text—that is, he has developed "metacognition," or the ability to understand and monitor his own comprehension. The reader can now select texts for independent journeys, decoding and experiencing story without teacher intervention or support.

All children should have daily independent reading experiences—even in kindergarten. Not only do they provide a kind of practice time, but they also lay the groundwork for developing a lifelong reading habit. To facilitate these experiences, teachers need to develop large classroom libraries that provide a wide variety of books from which children can select. It is through such choice that students develop a commitment to and love of reading. Fortunately, we now know that there is no lower age limit for these individual experiences. Many of us have seen preschoolers creating wonderful stories as they move through the pictures in a favorite book.

Students can be encouraged in their independent reading in several ways. Often after reading a work by a particular author or a text on a particular subject, readers have the background and motivation to move on to other works by that same author or other books concerning the same subject. That is, they have developed a schema for a particular textual experience. A reader's schema base becomes the support for independent reading. Teachers can provide the resources, pathways, and impetus for experiences of this kind. Opportunities that steep readers in particular topics, authors, and genres contribute to such a schema base; classroom libraries stocked with the necessary related texts allow students to explore and develop that base.

Once the tools have been provided, teachers must ensure that students have ample opportunities to use them. Many researchers have found that the great majority of students do very little reading outside of school. Accordingly, encouraging independent reading of self-selected literature in the classroom may provide some students with the only sustained reading time they ever have. In the 1970s, Lyman Hunt suggested a period be set aside each day for such reading, naming the activity Sustained Silent Reading. SSR, as it is usually called, will not only bring youngsters to story but also help establish lifetime reading habits. It is a lasting gift every teacher can provide.

Of course, we should also strive to encourage students to read *outside* the classroom. Any reading not planned for by the teacher could be termed "recreational reading." This is the reading done by members of a literate society, and our ultimate goal continues to be helping children become active participants in that society. Very often schools develop programs, often involving parents or other caregivers, that encourage recreational reading. Some businesses even take part in efforts to promote this kind of reading, offering rewards and incentives for reading a certain number of books. Yet the intrinsic value of reading does not come from programs and prizes—it comes from the pleasure of choosing and savoring a good book in one's free time. The literate professional demonstrates daily the importance of reading. As such professionals, we must actively show children that we read ourselves, for a variety of purposes and from a variety of texts. These demonstrations, perhaps more than anything else, can stimulate a desire in our students that can only be satisfied by story.

And so it is that teachers on the journey toward new and better literacy instruction base instructional practices on a variety of approaches that fulfill needs as they arise. Any of these approaches can be used with any story. In fact, it is easy to see how *all* readers, depending upon their development and the text used, will at some time need a supportive approach. Consequently, although these approaches have been described under the heading of the reading act, each can be modified to find its way into prereading (to prepare) or postreading (to extend, satiate, and celebrate).

Postreading

When was the last time you saw an adult doing a comprehension ditto after reading a piece of text? Most people do other things after reading. If it's a thought-provoking book or article, they share it with another person in some way. If it's a recipe, they make the cake. If it's an instruction manual, they build the model. If it's a letter, they respond in writing.

Sometimes they simply think about the text, comparing it to other literary works or to circumstances within their own lives. These real purposes of reading are destroyed on the pages of dittos, workbooks, and interrogating computer screens, where "correct" answers designate an "accelerated reader."

LITERATURE CONVERSATIONS

One of the most exciting and interesting ways to celebrate the reading of text is through small group conversations. Although sitting and discussing something with others sounds like a very simple idea—certainly something that all of us do with ease each day—it is actually one of the most difficult activities to implement. Some of this difficulty stems from teachers having been steeped in traditional models of instruction, so that even when they are intent on changing their behaviors, they still find themselves running the show. Ironically, when we do attempt to facilitate students' conversations, we often find that the students look to us to ask the questions—questions that they then feel obliged to answer. Furthermore, students tend to feel that it is the teacher who holds the keys to the "answer kingdom."

My own story of the bumpy journey toward a new paradigm of instruction is probably little different from that of most others who have attempted this trip. However, the endeavor has helped me to see not only literature response but also "that place called school" through a different lens. Once I headed in that direction, the children and I found ourselves on the doorstep of something new and quite different whose essence I can only refer to as real community. Much of this I came to realize by videotaping our first attempts at classroom literature conversations. For me, watching those videos unveiled the controlled parameters within which I held the children and helped me see just how much I maintained ownership of what was said and when.

For students to construct their own meanings, bring forth their own topics for discussion, and respond to the comments and questions of others in a natural way is, indeed, a monumental accomplishment—for both the students and the teacher. Demonstrating your own responses to read-alouds using think-aloud strategies will provide a model of the way in which adults think about what they are reading. After a period of demonstration, teachers can begin inviting students into the response circle.

Children of Maplemere Elementary School meet in a literature conversation quad.

Once students become comfortable using a variety of response channels with teacher guidance, they are ready to move into smaller, more autonomous groups. To pave the way, the teacher can join each small literary community during the reading act, modeling how to respond on removable sticky notes. As students see their teacher reading and stopping occasionally to stick a note on a spot and jot a few words to serve as a mnemonic or remembering device, they, too, become drawn into the sport. Later, during the group's postreading conversation, they watch the teacher use these reminder messages to comment on particular parts of the text. Students could also use notebooks, journals, bookmarks, or chart paper to keep track of questions and thoughts about the text.

Eventually, when all the conversation hinges are oiled and everything is rolling along in an independent manner, the teacher, along with the students, can begin adding some structure to the workings of the group. If left to develop without a framework, literature discussion groups can grow boring or foster socially unacceptable behavior. To avoid this, teachers should provide structure to literature conversations so they support students as they travel toward deeper relationships with both classmates and literature. For example, students need to be made aware of how good listeners act and respond. They need to discuss eye contact, body language, honest response, equal opportunities, and such, and they need to decide how to make these things part of their conversations. The class can even develop a list of what they think are good manners and use it as an assessment tool for individuals, groups, or the teacher.

Of course, it is very helpful to have examples of quality literature conversations to serve as models of possible structures. For those just beginning this journey, however, student examples may be impossible to obtain. Videotaping conversations from the television can at least provide examples of interaction patterns, thereby helping students to sense what it looks (or even feels) like to be part of a conversation. Some teachers start their own after-school literature circle and are able to videotape their adult interactions to use as a model.

It also helps simply to discuss various response possibilities. Teachers can model avenues of thought and questions that might be asked about a piece of literature. There are many such avenues, including the following:

— author/illustrator style, technique, mood, character development, etc.—for example, "Did anyone ever notice how Robert Munsch uses exaggeration to develop humor in *Mud Puddle*?"
— characters' behavior, temperament, relationships, etc.—for example, "It seems that the main characters in *Stone Fox* and *Hatchet* are going through a struggle. I wonder why the author does that."
— genres—for example, "I wonder if we could develop *James and the Giant Peach* into a play?"
— time periods and settings—for example, "I wonder which things in *Little House in the Big Woods* could still happen today?"
— personal tastes—for example, "I like *Jumanji* better than *The Stranger* because I think *Jumanji* has a stronger story line."

- causes and results of events—for example, "Do you think that erupting volcanoes or an ice age caused the dinosaurs to become extinct?"
- the reader's own life—for example, "My life is so different from Julie's. I'm not sure I could have lived that way."
- information reported—for example, "This doesn't really sound believable to me because...."
- "what if's"—for example, "What if the people in the plane hadn't seen him?"
- "maybe's" or hypotheses—for example, "Maybe she's doing that because that's what her mother did to her."

The journey into literature conversations, though difficult, is one of the most wonderful gifts a teacher can give to students. It is through such explorations that students learn the real joys of reading. Educators who actually carry this journey to its destination will be overwhelmed by the level of questions that children ask and the extent of their inquiry. Children are able to see things we've never seen and construct avenues we would never have considered, if we would but only give them the chance. We all need to give our students the gift of their own voices by carving a place and time for literature conversations in our classrooms and by using narratives for rich conversation rather than for testing. Authors do not write stories as a source for measurement. Good books are meant to be shared, and what better way to do this than through a literature conversation? This, then, remains the richest postreading experience.

ADDITIONAL POSSIBILITIES

There are, of course, many other postreading activities that are certainly beneficial—especially when using expository text. Some books inspire the creation of murals, drama, letters to the author, storytelling, and so on, while others lend themselves to research projects involving other content areas. The vignettes presented later in this book demonstrate various ideas for extending text. But the most important thing to keep in mind is that postreading allows youngsters a time to revel in learning and in story. It is a time to extend, satiate, and motivate, a time when all language arts can

"Literature Study Grouping Structure" gives an overview of the way in which I use various grouping possibilities for activities and instruction.

The activities that follow present, first, possibilities for partners (Dynamic Duos) and then for small groups (Friends Together). Each section includes ideas for pre- and post-reading.

DYADS

In this grouping structure, the teacher can provide students the freedom of choosing their own partners or can partner students according to specific needs. Sometimes the latter is played out in a situation called "peer tutoring," whereby one more-able learner acts as a facilitator for a less-able learner. Keith Topping suggests that when we partner students in this way, perhaps the best pairing is of students whose abilities vary only slightly. In this way, the more-skilled student solidifies her understanding as she talks to and teaches the other student. And, obviously, the less-able student learns because she has individual help. Sometimes a great deal of mileage is gained simply by allowing friendships to drive the process.

SMALL GROUPS

The dynamics of small cooperative groups in the classroom are quite important in that they lay the groundwork for the real world, where people often have to collaborate to bring something to fruition. For instance, in most major companies, staff now work in teams, playing off one another's ideas, extending them, helping shape and execute them. Even in schools, teachers are encouraged to work together team-teaching, creating curricula, developing goals and assessment strategies, and interviewing new teacher candidates. Many schools include parents, administrators, and community members in these activities. If this is the manner in which we get things accomplished in the real world, why shouldn't it also work in the classroom? Furthermore, researchers Roger and David Johnson, citing a variety of studies, claim that "the need to talk about information and ideas rather than just think about them is one of the variables contributing to higher achievement. In addition to basic achievement, retention of information and the development of specific strategies are enhanced for all students by the cooperative interaction."

Meaningful Activities Support the Individual

For years, many educators played "Guess What I'm Thinking," and naive little youngsters attempted to fill in the blanks. To get help was considered cheating. To need help was considered weak. The same teachers who at a local supermarket would stop to help a distressed child would allow that same child to experience frustration as he struggled alone—sometimes to the point of tears—in their own classrooms. And what's even more sad is that many teachers did not allow other students to support a peer, silencing children with the all-too-familiar admonition, "Do your own work."

Fortunately, those days are behind many of us. Teachers and students alike now assume the role of classroom coaches, mentors, facilitators, and mediators. Children are learning that it takes *all* members to make the team strong.

Sometimes, however, there is a need for individual autonomy, although seldom completely independent of the group. At times the entire class may be working on a project that requires something from everyone, in which case individuals work independently on a specific piece for the interdependent whole. An outside observer might think that students in this situation fit very well into the old do-your-own-work model. The difference lies in the fact that these students know that their individual part is integral to the success of the group. They are not simply producing a piece of paper to be turned in to the teacher, corrected, and handed back. They also know that if they run into a "road block," someone will be available to lend a helping hand.

This interdependence between the whole and its parts creates what has been called a holonomy. Art Costa, a noted speaker, writer, and researcher in the area of student potential, working with Robert Garmston, suggests that it is time that educators begin thinking long and hard about adopting a holonomic model. They tell us that such structures provide "a rich and essential resource" for higher order thinking.

Activities that employ such a structure can be found in "Independent Activities with Pre- to Postreading Connections," beginning on page 73.

But looking beyond all of the academic achievement that holonomic structures promote, we should consider another aspect that is certainly just as important. Alfie Kohn explains, "If we had to pick a logical setting in which to guide children toward caring about, empathizing with, and helping other people, it would be a place where they would regularly come into contact with their peers and where some sort of learning is already taking place. The school is such an obvious choice...." In a world filled with violence and conflict, our schools owe it to our children to demonstrate the way in which caring communities can support their members and evolve peacefully.

Meaningful Activities Allow Choice

In each of the activities that follow, students have a choice of what they will do and how they will do it. Children are encouraged to construct their own meanings, to create, and even to move beyond parameters formerly set by the teacher.

Sometimes being a member of a group will limit a student's choices. In these cases, the choices are made by group consensus and not by the teacher alone, even when he is also a member of that group. But each group member experiences the satisfaction of ownership, and with that ownership comes commitment. This provides a far different—and more powerful—impetus for doing a task than "because the teacher says so," trying to be "a good little girl," or getting a top grade on a report card.

Meaningful Activities Are Founded on Real Life

This element is one of the most difficult to carry out consistently, for we teachers do so love cute activities. Unfortunately, cute is not always functional. That is, it may be cute to have students write letters to Goldilocks to scold her for going into the house of the three bears; however, students writing such letters will certainly not receive a reply—and isn't that what letter-writing is all about? Now, if they wrote a letter instead to Paul Galdone or Joy Cowley, perhaps they might receive something in return, thereby connecting the activity to real life.

In order to provide appropriate models, I have tried to build most of the included activities around a functional context. Obviously, however, a youngster's life will not be ruined if we sneak in a "cute idea" here or there.

Meaningful Activities Help Integrate the Curriculum

Our world continues to expand and change in a multitude of ways, and consequently the curriculum has become so vast that it is impossible for us to teach it in pieces and parts as we once did. We therefore look for overlapping areas and complementary content among the subjects, using the disciplines as lenses for different ways to view the world. Thus, we can study weather, for example, through an anthropological, archeological, or biological lens, each of which helps us to see the world in a different, yet valid way. An integrated curriculum reflects our integrated world and shows students how they can use literacy processes to support those connections.

In the activities that follow, particularly in the last chapter, a variety of curricular areas (literature, science, social studies, mathematics) are supported by a variety of literacy processes (reading, writing, listening, speaking, viewing, numeracy, music, drawing, sculpting, movement, drama). Such an approach celebrates numerous learning channels and gives students of varied talents opportunities to grow and demonstrate their unique abilities.

Meaningful Activities Provide Assessment Data

Along with each of the following activities I have included suggestions for assessment. The suggestions are rooted in methods of "authentic" or "performance" assessment—that is, an approach that evaluates students' ongoing performance in real classroom situations—and will therefore provide grist for teachers whose districts are developing curricular standards of performance. Such assessment is often interpreted with reference to "benchmarks," which are rungs on a ladder of improvement, and allows for a student's progress to be explained through sets of well-defined goals.

Such benchmarks are often described through rubric scales, which have long been used in writing assessment. The knowledge and processes required to demonstrate performance at each level on a three- to five-point scale are described in a manner that allows teachers, students, and parents to understand "what it takes" for a piece of work to achieve a below average, average, or above average rating. For example, a primary class and their teacher, Heather Graffam, developed a four-point rubric scale to assess performance on a webbing activity. To earn a four, a web was required to be complete and use interesting words and art, among other things, while a one indicated frequent misspellings and messiness. With scales such as this, students understand what they must do to develop a high-quality piece. In fact, most can use them to rate their own work.

January Book Project Rubric

Where does your character web fall on our scale?

4: You used interesting describing words. You used art to help your work shine.

3: You followed directions. You had neat writing. You used good describing words.

2: You missed some directions. You misspelled words and/or used plain describing words.

1: Your work could be neater. You misspelled words from our Word Wall or from the book.

A rubric scale from Heather Graffam's class

Increasingly, assessment is carried out by evaluating a collection of student work, rather than performance on a specific task. These collections, along with their attached rubric scales, are often maintained by students themselves, in their personal "portfolios."

The inclusion of rubrics allows anyone who views the portfolio—even years later—to know the standard by which the work was assessed. I have found two kinds of portfolios particularly useful. In "working" portfolios, students can keep ongoing work to serve as examples of progress. Later, we select the best of this material to be placed into a student's "show" or "traveling" portfolio. This portfolio demonstrates a more cumulative perspective and travels with the child throughout his school experiences.

Although I share a variety of avenues for performance assessment, when and how any collection is done is a decision to be made locally. Regardless of local requirements, however, teachers will still need tools with which they can collect data describing a student's formative (ongoing) and summative (cumulative) progress. Samples of student work, checklists, and logs of various sorts can all serve these purposes. My colleagues and I also collect written running records as children share books with partners, and our students keep literary journals to write about their experiences with text. In addition, I have found that videotaping provides a very authentic means by which to collect data. For example, once a month, primary teachers at the elementary school where I now teach videotape an oral reading by each of their students. In this manner they accumulate a year-long running video log of (1) the reading behaviors of each student within a challenging piece of text, (2) the strategies that each student accesses to decode the text, and, occasionally, (3) a retelling of that piece of text for comprehension assessment. Teachers then work alone and in teams to assess and interpret the taped data into a written form. We also sometimes videotape children's performances of plays, presentations, and so on, which can be shared during parent-teacher conferences. Because one purpose of this performance data is to log an individual's progress in attaining various benchmarks, the footage is always captured at a time when the child is doing her best. In other words, it is as positive, yet realistic, as possible at that given time.

Although the activities that follow can easily be integrated into interdisciplinary units, the suggestions for assessment tend to focus primarily on student performance in a particular area of literacy as it is used *within* an interdisciplinary curriculum. It should be noted, however, that prototype activities could easily be revised to focus on other literacy processes and thereby yield different assessment data. Similarly, because the activities span subject areas, assessment could be developed that would be more global in nature. All of the preceding discussion has focused on assessing the student. In closing, I'd like to suggest that we also consider *self* and *program* assessment and, just as important, invite students and parents into the assessment process.

Introduction to Meaningful Activities

The next chapters present the heart of this book—the collection of activities itself. Each activity contains specific elements. Besides the literature suggestions and assessment ideas already mentioned, I provide a listing of the materials needed. I have found that preparing such a list helps the day flow in a more organized manner—and it avoids having to send a mid-morning messenger down to another classroom to borrow things such as rolling pins, an old newspaper, gray plasticene, and a large, heavy rock. Although the pressures of time may tempt us to omit this materials section from our planning, the inclusion of it results in a less-frazzled teacher, probably with fewer gray hairs.

The activities themselves are described very briefly and then presented through a vignette designed to demonstrate just how that activity might look in a classroom. I think of these vignettes as providing a "bird's eye view," for indeed, I hope that readers will feel as if they are small birds perched in some corner of the classroom, observing the comings and goings of its inhabitants. With these little language stories it was my intention to add the flavor of classroom life to methodology. This will be especially helpful to the preservice or new teacher, as well as adding spice for all of us who enjoy a little story. In most cases, the vignettes represent only a slice of that school day, but we must remember that they always fit into a larger context. In some cases I allude to that larger context; in others I do not.

Each vignette evolves through three phases: a beginning, middle, and end. I like to think of its beginning in terms of the "pre-activity" and its end as the "postactivity," while the middle of each little story usually presents students in a more autonomous and constructing phase. The pre-activity part of any lesson has been dubbed many things by many people—from "anticipatory set" to "modeling"—and for every name there are a variety of understandings regarding what should be done in the period before the students take over. In this book, the pre-activity prepares the students for their own participation, and thus often includes some kind of modeling, support, and encouragement. The goal is that after this part of each activity, students will be able to handle the task with a minimal amount of help. In this way, teachers will be able to work with other groups, feeling confident that constructive involvement is taking place in other areas of the classroom. Totally involved students are rarely the discipline problems that bored children are. So actually, everything else rests on this initial step—if it is a success, the remainder of the activity will probably also be a success. I have found it important not to rush through this part. If it's a week of assemblies, school pictures, and Santa's Secret Workshop, better to limit the post- than the pre-activities.

The consummation of each activity usually involves some kind of sharing or celebration. In my experience, we accomplished this through publishing, posting, and performing, or by actually using the process or product in some way. Postactivities are important and students need always to be able to count on this sharing or using time. Anticipating such times can motivate students throughout the task. The activities, therefore, have meaning and are carried out for a good reason—not just so students can stuff a paper into a book bag, take it home, and then throw it away over the weekend.

I hope the following activities will provide support as we all attempt to create more meaningful and caring environments for children in our classrooms.

MEANINGFUL ACTIVITIES

TO REPLACE SEATWORK

Skill and information about materials, tools, and laws of
energy are acquired while activities are carried on for their
own sake. The fact that they are socially representative gives
a quality to the skill and knowledge gained which makes
them transferable to out-of-school situations.

John Dewey

. . . .

DYNAMIC DUOS

> When I receive the other, I am totally with the other. The
> relation is for the moment exactly as Buber has described
> it.... The other "fills the firmament."
>
> Nel Noddings

Prereading Activities

T he following activities are designed to motivate
students to undertake the reading act and to support them as
they do so. Therefore, each Activity is actually a "preActivity"
that, in this chapter, is executed with a partner.

STORYTELLING TO ORGANIZE WRITING

ACTIVITY: *Do knee-to-knee folk and fairy tale storytelling; create
illustrated version*
TEXT: *Hans Christian Andersen, The Ugly Duckling*
ASSESSMENT: *Observe children's storytelling and log presence of
beginning, middle, and end*
MATERIALS: *White paper, pencils, crayons*

As Mrs. Nye settles one group of students into their task, she
invites the group that is going to read *The Ugly Duckling* to a
carpeted corner of the room. She introduces the topic of fairy
tales, saying "When I read fairy tales there are some common
elements I watch for. Good versus evil seems to be a part of
every fairy tale. Can you think of anything else that connects
fairy tales into a genre?" After a brief discussion, Mrs. Nye
and the students decide that frequently fairy tales involve
the numbers three and seven, are introduced by "Once upon
a time," often have characters that are royalty, and include

fantastic or magical elements. Abdul then suggests, "I know a fairy tale that has lots of those things—'Cinderella'!" Abdul's contribution gives rise to suggestions from others. Comparisons abound.

Mrs. Nye then suggests, "How about choosing a partner to do a knee-to-knee storytelling of a fairy tale that both of you know?" As each child sits cross-legged with knees touching those of his partner, the teacher walks through the group listening to the versions. She quickly decides that her time could be better spent working with another group across the room. When she notices that most of the storytelling group seems finished, however, Mrs. Nye returns and calls for a pair to tell their version of a story to the others. She then invites the students to move with their partners to another place in the room where they can work together illustrating their version. She suggests that before they start drawing, they turn up the bottom of each blank page to reserve a spot for a caption. Sean is heard saying to Maurice, "You do the writing and I'll do the drawing. Come on!" Later each pair's pages are stapled into book form and shared with others. A few children decide to place their drafts in their writing folders to develop later during writers' workshop.

GETTING A HEAD START

ACTIVITY: *Read first few pages of story with a partner*
TEXT: *Paul Galdone, The Little Red Hen; Charles Dickens, A Christmas Carol*
ASSESSMENT: *Observe and log cueing strategies of readers*
MATERIALS: *None*

Miss Williams knows that her primary students need support to move through text early in the year, so she has decided to rely on predictable books. She has discovered that although many such books contain repetitive structures, their beginnings often do not adhere closely to the pattern. Consequently, she decides to invite students to "use" a partner until they get the hang of the pattern. Miss Williams calls a group forward, introduces the text, and draws the children's attention to patterns they might find in it. "We've read many books with patterns that help us get through the story," she says. "Now we have another one, and I'll bet many of you already know some of the patterns for this story. How many of you have heard *The Little Red Hen* before?"

While anxious hands flutter in the air, some children begin interjecting anecdotes related to their own experiences with the story. Soon several have suggested some of the obvious patterns: the "Not I" sections and "Then I'll do it myself" parts, and also the predictable sequence of planting. "Come sit close," invites Miss Williams, "and as I read aloud, perhaps you'd like to join in on some of the patterned parts."

After Miss Williams shares the book, she asks the children to move to another part of the room where, working with a partner, they can help each other through the text until each feels comfortable enough to venture into more independent reading. The teacher meanders through the partners for a few minutes and then invites another group to meet for sharing, since they have finished their prereading project.

IDENTIFYING VOCABULARY

ACTIVITY: *Using discussion and a variety of reference sources, find meanings for words on a vocabulary list*
TEXT: *Theodore Taylor, The Cay*
ASSESSMENT: *Collect vocabulary list to log and assess students' sources of reference*
MATERIALS: *Dictionaries, encyclopedia, atlas, duplicated word lists*

(Although this vignette is directed toward the teaching of meaning vocabulary at the intermediate level, for the primary grades the Activity could be adapted to focus on decoding sight vocabulary.)

Mr. Peczkowski's classroom is full of displays: student work, charts giving examples of genre elements and types of punctuation, lists related to the latest thematic study, and so on. This is an active place! Every student seems consumed either in an endeavor with a peer or in an activity that keeps her alone in her little part of the classroom world.

Mr. Peczkowski announces that he'd like to see those students who signed up to be in a play based on *The Cay*. He tells them that when they're reading their books, they will come across vocabulary integral to the story's meaning, and if they do not understand these words, they may misinterpret the text. He indicates that he has prepared a vocabulary list and asks students to sit with their designated partners to discuss the words and their possible meanings. If students cannot construct meaning for a given word, they are invited to check in dictionaries, an atlas, the class set of encyclopedias, and other references on CD-ROM. Just as the children are about to begin the task, their teacher adds, "Oh, and beside each of the words, let me know how you came to find out about that one—dictionary, encyclopedia, whatever—and initial it to show who was responsible for each particular word. If you both initial, that's fine, too."

Susan responds, "How much time do we have?"

Mr. Peczkowski suggests that they meet in a half-hour to discuss some of the words whose meanings may still be eluding them. This gives him time to sit in on a literature circle that has begun in the far corner of the room.

RESEARCHING THE SETTING

ACTIVITY: *Research the setting of a story*
TEXT: *Lynn Cherry, The Great Kapok Tree; Mark Helprin, Swan Lake*
ASSESSMENT: *Assess pair interaction through individual questionnaires completed after the activity*
MATERIALS: *Library books related to topic and text setting*

Mrs. Kavanaugh stumbles into the classroom laden with a variety of texts, all related to ecology and the state of the planet. As the bell rings, several eight-year-olds rush in, proudly displaying their own copies of books on this topic. Visitors can read the excitement on the faces of teacher and children as they share what they've found for their theme study. Late arrivals gather 'round. Tommy hands Mrs. Kavanaugh a newspaper clipping describing the destruction of a rain forest in South America, so Mrs. Kavanaugh decides that it is a good time to introduce the topic of rain forests and a related text, *The Great Kapok Tree* . After Tommy shares his article with the class, Mrs. Kavanaugh goes on to add some more information, using a large map of the world to show where the remaining rain forests are located. Students start to offer ideas for many activities they could undertake that would relate to their study of this topic, but Mrs. Kavanaugh suggests that before they create ecology "awareness posters" to display in their community or write a letter to the newspaper, it would help if they gained a little more background. So, she and the students begin to discuss some of the books they have brought into the room.

Suda offers to share the newspaper and magazine articles she has been collecting on this topic for the past two years. The class seems especially interested in Suda's personal commitment to the rain forests, and many children gather around hoping to begin their research by delving into her private collection. Noticing their interest, Mrs. Kavanaugh suggests, "This might be a good time for some of you to begin your own collections. Why don't you find a partner to begin some research? You can use all the sources we've collected so far, and any others you can track down."

As she reaches for her clipboard, she feels happy that the group is so involved. This gives her a chance to work with Phillip and Betsy, both of whom might find computer cataloging of references a valuable tool for their research, but may need her help with the equipment.

INTERVIEWING TO BUILD BACKGROUND

ACTIVITY: *Conduct interviews with partners*
TEXT: *Judy Blume, The One in the Middle Is a Green Kangaroo; Katherine Paterson, Jacob, Have I Loved*
ASSESSMENT: *Assess performance in practice activity to determine who may need help prior to undertaking the main project*
MATERIALS: *Clipboards, paper, pencils*

Early in the school year, Miss Davis and her class decide it would be fun to learn about one another's families. The teacher smiles as she looks around the class and notes the diverse cultures represented. "This unit will have a lot of meaning for us," she tells the class. "It's wonderful that we have so many differences to celebrate."

Natasha, putting away materials from another Activity, looks up and asks, "Miss Davis, how do we get started studying our families?" After the class shares some suggestions, the idea of interviewing family members is put forward. Miss

Davis tells the children that it would probably be beneficial for them to practice before they begin the interviewing. The next story the class will be reading focuses on a family, and she describes a few of the character relationships. She then asks students to come forward to put their names on a chart, under the category that designates their placement among their siblings: oldest, middle, youngest, or only child. After all the children have done so, Miss Davis asks that they get their clipboards and some paper and select a partner to interview, but that they must choose someone whose name is in a different column from their own. She suggests that they might want to start with the question "How does it feel to be the youngest (or oldest, or "middlest," or an only child)?" She hopes that later the students will be able to draw some conclusions as they share with the class the information they have collected.

While the children settle into their favorite spots with their partners, Miss Davis invites the other literature group to an area of the room where Myra and Martie have been busily clearing a spot for the creation of a mural.

Postreading Activities

The following situations again involve working with partners. However, the activities in this section are carried out after the reading act. They can be thought of as the icing on the cake.

RETELLING

ACTIVITY: *Retell story knee-to-knee; create illustrated version for literary journal and to share with others*
TEXT: *Pat Hutchins, The Doorbell Rang; Doris Smith, A Taste of Blackberries*
ASSESSMENT: *Record anecdotal notes on students' retellings; assess literary journal picture sequences and copy quality entries for portfolios*
MATERIALS: *Literary journals (bought or made)*

A group of students sits together on a frayed rug in one corner of their old, but pleasant, classroom. The teacher has just finished sharing a book with the group and several students are beginning to mention the parts they liked best. To provide an opportunity for the children to discuss a story with a strong and logical sequence and to encourage them to think about its temporal aspects, Mrs. Gallo asks them to sit knee-to-knee with a partner and together retell the story. To get them all off to a confident start, she asks, "What was the first thing that happened?"

She then moves about the group as partners talk their way through the story. She stops here and there to commend those who are re-creating successfully. Occasionally she hesitates for a moment to jot a note or two on a sheet attached to a small clipboard. On other days when Mrs. Gallo uses this technique, she chooses to let retellings proceed without her so that she can act as facilitator for other groups.

As a follow-up to the retelling, Mrs. Gallo invites each student to put four story-pictures in his journal: one for the beginning, two for the middle, and one for the end of the story. Students then share their work to see which parts others selected to draw.

SUPPORTING A STANCE

ACTIVITY: *Match students holding opposite opinions for a discussion; students log points of dispute in writing to share later*
TEXT: *Bernard Waber, Ira Sleeps Over; Natalie Babbit, Tuck Everlasting*
ASSESSMENT: *Make anecdotal records logging social interactions and manner in which problems are solved*
MATERIALS: *Chart paper, ink marker, literary journals (bought or made)*

(This is a hybrid pre- and postreading Activity. It is conducted part way through a story and provides a foundation, as well as an incentive, for reading the next part.)

The students have just been asked to stop reading, after finishing approximately half the story. From the looks on their faces, it's clear that any one of them might complain, "But it's just getting to the good part!" Mr. Frizelle asks a few questions: "How many of you would have said that? Done that? Felt like that?" He is trying to take inventory of varying opinions that demonstrate sympathy for one character or another. From his knowledge of the class and from the information he gleans during his questioning, he tries to match partners who hold diverse opinions, suggesting that they discuss until the two can resolve their differences. He goes on to say, "Obviously there are no 'rights' or 'wrongs,' only opinions that you've got to support. I'll jot down some of the ways I hear you backing up your ideas as I listen in on your discussions," and he holds up his clipboard to symbolize his intent. "Then I'll share these with you later." Knowing that some of these discussions could provoke heated arguments, he adds, "If you and your partner really can't agree or find some compromise, I would suggest that you put your feelings into words in your literary journals, so that we can discuss the issue later with the whole group." During discussions, only one pair needs to be reminded to use the journals.

When the partner discussions begin to wane, Mr. Frizelle invites the group to gather in a circle on the carpet in the back of the room. As students try to settle issues related to character traits, Abigail suggests that it would be interesting to develop a list of all the traits they've noticed. Mr. Frizelle reaches for a piece of chart paper, saying, "That's a good idea, Abigail. And then when we finish the story we can review the attributes of each character and see if any of them changed in the second half."

ALTERNATIVE VIEWPOINTS

ACTIVITY: *One partner develops a list of story's sad times, while the other develops a list of happy times*
TEXT: *Rosemary Wells, Noisy Nora; Barbara Robinson, The Best Christmas Pageant Ever*
ASSESSMENT: *Collect lists to assess comprehension of story*
MATERIALS: *Paper, pencils*

Ms. Garan has just finished the prereading Activity for the group's story and is about to partner a strong reader with a weaker one for the reading act. First, however, she holds up two pieces of paper, one labeled "Sad Times" and the other "Happy Times." The students listen as their teacher explains that stories often have a mixture of happy and sad situations.

She demonstrates using a well-known story, saying, "We know that in 'Snow White,' it was a sad time when Snow White was poisoned, but it was a happy time when she was kissed by the prince, right? What other parts of 'Snow White' can you think of that might fall into one of these categories?" Students begin suggesting other sad and happy times, which the teacher transcribes on the chart. Quite a list develops, along with some disagreement on a few events—which end up being placed in both categories! Ms. Garan knows that it is from activities such as this that students come to understand point of view.

Later, when partners finish reading the story, Ms. Garan invites each dyad to decide who will list (or draw) the happy times and who will focus on the sad. As the students reread and write together, Ms. Garan checks on them a couple of times but concentrates on introducing a prereading Activity to another group. She later suggests that students hold their happy and sad times lists until the next day, so that they can discuss the results with their whole group.

GOOD-BAD-QUESTIONABLE

ACTIVITY: *List "good," "bad," and "questionable" elements of story, addressing events, characters, author's style, etc.*
TEXT: *Wanda Gag, Millions of Cats; Roald Dahl, Charlie and the Chocolate Factory*
ASSESSMENT: *Copy Good-Bad-Questionable pages for working portfolios; use rubric to log data on students' participation in whole-group discussion*
MATERIALS: *Duplicated Good-Bad-Questionable pages, pencils*

Miss Schott stands chatting with a colleague during the lunch hour before her class will be starting their new literature studies. "I can't wait for them to read the new stories because they're very controversial and I enjoy seeing how children think about the controversies," she says. "At first they don't get it. They just read the story and talk about the main points—that's it. But when I say that I can see some parts of the story that are really kind of bad or unpleasant and others that I tend to wonder about, then the kids start thinking, too. I'm going to try a new approach today. I'll let you know how it goes."

Later that day, after Miss Schott has talked about this idea with a group of students, she invites partners to work together to put their thoughts down on paper. She gives each pair a sheet titled "Good-Bad-Questionable" and divided into three columns, explaining that characters, events, settings, things in the author's style, and so on can be noted under the appropriate headings. She then makes sure that everyone is off to a positive start before she moves on to work with another group.

Later Miss Schott collects all the Good-Bad-Questionable papers and copies the entries under the "Questionable" heading onto a large chart, which the group can use as an impetus for discussion the next time they meet. She has already decided that Mario would make a good leader for this Activity and has jotted him an invitation to serve in this capacity.

DRAMATIZING DUOS

ACTIVITY: *One partner makes puppets while the other tape-records the play; they then practice together and perform for audience*
TEXT: *Robert Munsch, The Paper Bag Princess; Scott O'Dell, Island of the Blue Dolphins*
ASSESSMENT: *Collect peer assessment of plays to summarize for portfolio; videotape of performance*
MATERIALS: *Construction paper, yarn, paint, glue, audiotapes, tape recorders, video camera, videotape*

Before the students in the literature group begin reading, Mrs. Shea suggests that they focus particularly on the characters, with the idea that they will later work in pairs to create a puppet play version of the story. When they have finished reading, Mrs. Shea calls students to the art center, where she has laid out a variety of materials. She invites the students to pair off and develop a plan so that together each duo can create a taped retelling of the story (or parts of it) and puppets to dramatize it.

Most students decide to work on each Activity together; however, a few decide that one of the pair will do the puppets while the other tape-records. Mrs. Shea borrowed tape recorders from two other teachers so that students wouldn't become impatient, but she suggests that they can practice their puppet movements if they do have to wait for a machine. Most students have had experience using tape recorders, but those who haven't learn from their peers. Several students who finish taping quickly join their partners to work on the puppets, while others decide to enhance their plays in other ways, such as by constructing scenery. Then Joey, who is always thinking ahead, suggests that perhaps they could write letters to other teachers asking to perform for their classes. There is unanimous agreement, so the students begin the letters.

The project takes a few days, but the students are so involved that Mrs. Shea can focus on other literature groups. When the pairs are ready to perform for the class, she borrows a video camera so the children can share their plays with their families and add another piece to their growing portfolios of performance.

ACTIVITY: *One partner reads while the other dramatizes character through mime*
TEXT: *Esphyr Slobodkina, Caps for Sale; Mark Twain, The Adventures of Tom Sawyer*
ASSESSMENT: *Record video footage of mime interpretations (if video cameras are not available, anecdotal notes can be made)*
MATERIALS: *None*

After the students have finished reading, Miss March tells them that one of her favorite things about the story is that the characters are very animated. She explains, "There are lots of things you can do when you've read a lively story: you might make a cartoon version, compare it to a time when you've acted that way, or dramatize it in one way or another." She then goes on to explain mime and demonstrates by miming how to make a sandwich. Again and again she repeats, "You must exaggerate your movements. It feels funny, but it looks great!"

Miss March then invites some students to mime various activities. She later partners stronger students with weaker ones and asks that one child read while the other mimes the story. She suggests they take turns with these roles, and mentions that she will be moving among the dyads videotaping so that they can later enjoy one another's interpretations.

After a while the room grows quite noisy with so many readers, so finally the teacher suggests that perhaps a couple of pairs would like to move into the hall. This helps the noise level a bit. But it seems that Miss March was more disturbed than the children were, for they are all so engrossed in their own activities that only a few glance around to observe the mimes and readers who are leaving the classroom!

. . . .

FRIENDS TOGETHER

Communities do not ask "How can we justify taking this person in?" Instead the question is "Is it at all justifiable to keep this person out?"

M. Scott Peck

Prereading Activities

In these activities, students work together in groups of three to six members. The vignettes describe classroom situations designed to ground the reading act.

DEVELOPING SETTING THROUGH A MURAL

ACTIVITY: *After discussion, develop mural of story setting*
TEXT: *June Melser and Joy Cowley, In a Dark, Dark Wood; Gary Paulsen, Hatchet*
ASSESSMENT: *Photocopy picture of mural for portfolio, under which student notes the portion she created*
MATERIALS: *Corkboard or other display area, butcher paper, construction paper, scissors, glue, painting supplies, other materials suggested by students*

It's Monday and the class is quite excited for they are about to start their new literature studies. Each group will be reading a different text, and several students waver between which book they'd like to experience and which friends they'd like to work with. Finally, Mrs. Hensal calls the first group to the meeting area, a kind of island amid tables, chairs, bookcases, and easels. She explains that the story they will read has a strong and important setting—that is, the setting really makes the story. To build a foundation, she describes the setting, and the students begin to interact, reflecting on forests they've visited. Their teacher then suggests that it would be fun to start a mural that the group could add to as the story unfolds. Mrs. Hensal had arrived earlier than usual that morning so she could gather materials for the mural. The collection now sits on a table beside a large corkboard divider covered with brown butcher paper upon which students can paste their cut-outs, paint, or draw. To allay chaos, Mrs. Hensal suggests that they first work together to list some things they would like to include on the mural, and then each student could sign up to be responsible for one item. Before leaving the group, the teacher asks Shantelle to put an appropriate tape in the recorder to help develop a mood as they work. Shantelle slides *Sounds of Nature* into the tape recorder, but waits to press "Play" until the list is finished.

As these students get started, Mrs. Hensal begins a prereading activity with another group. At the end of their work period, the mural group is anxious to move into the story to see how they might extend their artwork.

CREATING A LIST

ACTIVITY: *Develop a list of categories related to story's main topic*
TEXT: *Mary Ann Hoberman, A House Is a House for Me; Steven Kellogg, Can I Keep Him?*
ASSESSMENT: *Review group chart to note group harmony and member interdependence*
MATERIALS: *Large chart paper, ink markers*

"How many of you have a pet?" asks Miss Wendland. "And how many of you would like to have a pet?" Almost every hand in the group shoots into the air. "What kind of pets are there?" she asks the students.

The children call out several pets—hamsters, dogs, cats, guinea pigs, snakes, fish....

"We could probably continue for quite some time on this," admits Miss Wendland, "but let's look at one kind of animal and see if we can do the same thing again. Let's try kinds of dogs." The teacher and children sit for another five minutes thinking of kinds of dogs, and then cats and fish. Then Miss

Wendland tells the group that the story they will be reading is about houses, a topic that can also be subcategorized. After selecting a scribe, who receives a large piece of chart paper and an ink marker, the teacher asks the group to move to a less populated area of the room to develop a "Kinds of Houses" list. She explains that later they will be able to compare what they've come up with to the houses in the story. She adds, "Please initial each one you add so that we can make sure everyone is getting a chance." As Miss Wendland meets the needs of another group, she continues to check on the houses group occasionally. They work diligently for about a half-hour, at which time the list covers all of the front and part of the back of the paper. They are excited to share what they've created, and also to read their text to discover if they've thought of all the houses. As Jill leaves the room that afternoon, she sticks her head back in long enough to say, "I just thought of another one, Miss Wendland. Can I add it? Pl-ea-ea-se?"

In my own multi-age classroom in Lockport, children learned to collaborate in constructing text, while a scribe transcribed their dictation.

TAPED BACKGROUNDS

ACTIVITY: *Listen to a taped version of a printed text and create illustration of main idea*
TEXT: *Robert Munsch, Thomas's Snowsuit; Joni Mitchell and Alan Baker, Both Sides Now*
ASSESSMENT: *Collect drawings to assess interpretation of main idea*
MATERIALS: *Commercially produced audiotape of text, tape recorder*

"There are a variety of ways to enjoy a story," Mr. Rizzo explains to the anxious faces before him. "Some authors interpret their stories through words on the pages of a book, but other authors interpret them out loud, through storytelling or even singing. What story songs do you know?"

Students volunteer a variety of story songs, from current pop tunes to childhood favorites such as "Jack and Jill." After several responses, Mr. Rizzo inserts, "Before we experience today's wonderful story from the pages of a book, let's experience it another way. Find a comfortable position, relax, and enjoy. Jason, you can be in charge of on, off, and rewind. After you listen to the tape once, it might be fun to start a drawing of the main idea while you listen again. When the story's over the second time, finish the picture and jot a caption underneath. We'll share your interpretations later."

Mr. Rizzo makes certain everyone is ready to listen before moving on to a group of students who are just about finished reading a story independently.

COMPARING NEWSPAPER STYLES

ACTIVITY: *Select a news medium to analyze and examine its reporting of a current event*
TEXT: *Examples of various media*
ASSESSMENT: *Using a rubric scale, rate each student's performance as related to voice, eye contact, content, and visuals (or have students rate one another using a class-created scale)*
MATERIALS: *Variety of newspapers, magazines, video recorder, tape recorder, television*

An incident that received wide media coverage gave rise to daily discussions and debates in Mr. Guillaume's class. Students again and again stated their opinions, usually beginning, "Well, I read," "I heard," "I saw...." This spurred Mr. Guillaume to suggest, "Since most of you seem interested in what's going on, why don't we try to find out more about it and see if we can figure out how different media influence the knowledge we're receiving. Have any of you noticed that the news is reported in different ways through different sources?"

This provoked more discussion, and then Jillian suggested, "Couldn't we see how a bunch of different places report? Like, how the TV does it, how the radio does it, how the newspaper does it?" "Sounds like a good idea to me," agreed Mr. Guillaume. "Let's develop a list of media first." As he grabbed a large piece of chart paper, students began dictating: "TV, newspapers, magazines...." Afterwards, members of the class signed up for the medium of their choice. To provide a common structure for the groups, Mr. Guillaume suggested, "Why doesn't each group start by simply thinking about a variety of facets of your particular medium. For instance, if you selected magazines, you might talk about the kinds of magazines there are out there, and then look to see how different ones are organized. For instance, there are some magazines that have a lot of pictures—like *National Geographic*. But others report news events or offer a lot of opinions."

After the groups had discussed aspects of their various media, their teacher suggested that they bring in examples of the different ways the news event was being covered within their medium. "There will have to be some volunteers from the TV and radio groups to video- or tape-record a few segments, OK? But try to plan it a bit first, so you'll agree on what to tape."

The groups met each day for a brief period to discuss what they'd found and to analyze how the coverage differed from example to example. This generated so much excitement that Mr. Guillaume suggested, "Next week, why doesn't each group present what they've found? The newspaper group could start off on Monday, and then maybe the radio group could present on Tuesday, and so on.

Remember to bring in as many examples as possible to share. And then on Friday we could talk as a class about how your opinions might have changed as a result of your analyzing the media."

This idea was met with such enthusiasm that Mr. Guillaume agreed to invite the other upper grade classes to attend the presentations.

ORGANIZING WRITTEN INFORMATION

ACTIVITY: *Collect a variety of printed information concerning local attractions and organize it according to categories*
TEXT: *Travel and tourist brochures from local attractions, local newspapers*
ASSESSMENT: *Log contributions made by each student*
MATERIALS: *Large chart paper, ink markers*

As the school year wound up, Mrs. Keiling's students began to share the activities they and their families had planned for the vacation. Some of these were going to take students across the country or beyond, while others would occur right in their own backyards. Desmond had brought in an advertising brochure from a local amusement park and was eagerly sharing his family's plans to visit it. Mrs. Keiling saw an opportunity to explore a rich and exciting area for research, so she decided to "piggyback" off Desmond's example. "With summer coming, there could be opportunities for all of you to take in special activities," she said. "Not me," grumped Ann. "We don't have a car anymore."

"Oh, but Ann, you don't need a car for many of the things our area has to offer. I bet we'd all be surprised to discover just how much there is to do this summer that even I don't know about," Mrs. Keiling responded.

"Yeah! I bet none of you knew there's an old cemetery down by the river that has graves that are over 200 years old!" shouted Erin. "Wow, I'd like to take my camera down there, Erin," Mrs. Keiling replied. "OK, so why don't we start by just thinking of all the places or activities that we know of—just off the tops of our heads. Then we can bring in information from brochures, newspapers, and such that will expand our list."

Mrs. Keiling knew of quite a few places where the students could find printed information about their area, and asked if some students might like to volunteer to call the tourist information center, automobile club, city hall, and other agencies.

With the groundwork laid, Mrs. Keiling suggested that the class needed a way to organize the information once it started coming in, and she called for some ideas. After a brief discussion, the students decided to categorize by type of activity, location, cost, and time required. Mrs. Keiling then proposed that everyone could select the group to which they wanted to belong. "Groups will have to decide how they want to organize within their category. For instance, if you choose 'Cost,' you'll probably want to begin with 'Free.' But then, will you group by 'Under Five Dollars' or 'Under One Dollar?' Each group will have to make these kinds of decisions within some sort of organizational plan. Or does anyone have a better idea?"

Toby said that he figured they could just write the price of the activity down. "I don't see any need to put 'Under Five Dollars.'" A few students came up with other ideas, and the groups each began to discuss the merits of the various suggestions. Finally, a decision was made by consensus, and the groups started work on constructing an organizational plan for the information they would begin perusing the next day. Over the coming days, the students would read the material, discuss it, and then write out the pertinent details on chart paper for display.

Three weeks later the class had discovered so much information about their area and their charts were all so full that Janelle came up with a grand idea: "Hey, why don't we make a little book to put in libraries and places like that, and in it we could write about everything we've found out."

"What a fantastic idea!" agreed Mrs. Keiling. "Why keep all this good information to ourselves?"

Postreading Activities

Reading is a recursive process, and in the following vignettes the divisions between prereading, the reading act, and postreading begin to blur. In some, postreading discussions and research lead to new reading, while in others, discussion during the reading act encourages children to continue a book or to engage in more in-depth exploration of a text.

ACTIVITY: *Following teacher model, learn how to "wonder" through a story, laying the groundwork for literature discussion*
TEXT: *Patricia Reilly Giff, The Beast in Ms. Rooney's Room*
ASSESSMENT: *Note informally which students need to be "repartnered"*
MATERIALS: *None*

Mrs. DelMonte had discovered a great new book to read aloud: *The Beast in Ms. Rooney's Room* by Patricia Reilly Giff. She was excited about introducing this author to the class, for Giff has written many books, and Mrs. DelMonte hoped she could "hook" students with this read-aloud.

The teacher called the class to the carpet in the corner of the room and asked the students to sit with someone with whom they would like to share some thoughts. After the children were all seated, she asked, "Would everyone hold up the hand of his or her partner?" After settling a couple of partner issues, she began by touching on the background of the author, mentioning that Giff's own experiences as a teacher provided grist for her stories. Mrs. DelMonte displayed a few other books by this author, suggesting that students might want to develop a literature study around some of them after she had finished reading *The Beast in Ms. Rooney's Room*.

Because she knew that her students were not yet very experienced in literature discussion, she started by modeling the way she wondered about a book as she began to read it: "I wonder what kind of beast *The Beast in Ms. Rooney's Room* is about. I also wonder if this is going to be a book about make-believe monsters. Probably not, because Patricia Reilly Giff usually writes about things that happen in real life." Mrs. DelMonte then began reading chapter one aloud. After a few paragraphs, she stopped, looked up at the students, and invited, "Turn to your partner, and share what you wonder about the story so far."

A few children did not respond immediately, either because they were thinking or were confused over what was expected. Mrs. DelMonte moved over to one student and reinforced with a special invitation: "Young-Hee, do you wonder about Richard Best? Do you wonder about his school? Do you wonder about Matthew's stick-out ears? Do you wonder what the author is trying to do? Share what you wonder."

Young-Hee turned to her partner and said, "I wonder about Matthew's stick-out ears."

After most of the students had shared, Mrs. DelMonte said, "Let's see if reading some more satisfies anybody's wonders." The teacher continued to read from where she had left off, stopping a few paragraphs later to invite, "Share with your partner what you wonder now."

Most of the students appeared very anxious to share, so, after a period of discussion, Mrs. DelMonte extended a broader invitation: "Who would like to share with the whole group what you just shared with your partner?"

Three students raised their hands. After each had contributed, Mrs. DelMonte suggested that the rest of the students turn to their own partners to share what they thought about what was said. The class continued to wonder through the story, and Mrs. DelMonte was happy to see that the children quickly became eager to discuss their thoughts and ideas. They were well on their way to independence in conversations about literature.

MAGAZINES AND NEWSPAPERS: A STEADY DIET

ACTIVITY: *Use sustained silent reading to provide impetus for discussion, research, and a class project*
TEXT: *Newspapers, magazines*
ASSESSMENT: *Log anecdotal notes describing the ways each student contributes to the project*
MATERIALS: *None*

It was sustained silent reading time, and one could almost hear a pin drop in Miss Stevenson's room. The students knew that discussion would follow this half-hour period of silent enjoyment of text, so if they had questions or comments they wanted to share, they wrote them down on sticky notes or in their literature logs for later reference.

As the familiar music of Handel signaled from the tape player, students quietly found good stopping places in their texts. When everyone seemed ready, Chris leaned over and turned off the music. After thanking Chris, Miss Stevenson remarked, "I noticed that several of you are reading newspaper or magazine articles about last week's terrible earthquake. Who has something about this that they would like to discuss?"

Several students raised their hands, so Miss Stevenson divided the class into small groups, inviting each of the interested individuals to join a group to share what he or she had learned through reading. Within minutes the groups became hubs for conversation. Later, when they met again as a whole class, Miss Stevenson asked, "Are there any thoughts you'd now like to draw to the whole group's attention?"

Edward seemed anxious to share: "You know, I really feel sorry for those people. It must be hard to be homeless. I read about one family that didn't have one thing left. What if they don't have any relatives around? What if they just moved there and they don't know anyone? What will they do?"

"The Red Cross usually helps," answered Angie. "I've seen them helping people on TV."

"Maybe we could do something," added Carolyn.

"Maybe we could get some things together and send them—like blankets and clothes and towels," Angie responded again.

"That sounds like a wonderful project for us," agreed Miss Stevenson.

"Maybe we could make a phone call to see what they need—" Then Jake interjected, "Yeah, and we can watch CNN tonight and I'll go on-line with my computer to see what I can find out on the web." "OK," the teacher went on, "why don't we all check sources tonight and come back tomorrow with as much information as possible. Then we can decide what the victims might need, where to send it, and such. Before you leave today, if you'd like to participate, please log your intentions for tonight's research on the chart over there. That way, everyone won't check the same source. And maybe you'd also like to look for things at home that you might be able to donate." For her part in the project, Miss Stevenson decided to provide the postage they'd need to mail the items they collected. She also decided to e-mail the local newspaper to ask for more information about agencies that were receiving donations. She jotted her idea regarding the e-mail on the chart.

ACTIVITY: *Plot points on a map as they are reached by a story character on a journey, and research the locations visited*
TEXT: *Vera B. Williams and Jennifer Williams, Stringbean's Trip to the Shining Sea; Karen Hesse, Letters from Rifka*
ASSESSMENT: *Place exemplary copies of student work in portfolios at project's completion*
MATERIALS: *Copies of master map, information on locations collected from on-line services or the Internet, automobile associations, travel bureaus, atlases, etc.*

Mrs. Hilwiller had finished reading aloud the first part of the book, and discussion now seemed to be waning. The students had talked about the geographic area where the story began, and the class appeared quite interested in tracking the characters' journey. The teacher knew that picking up on the children's lead often proved beneficial, so she suggested, "It might be fun to follow the characters as they travel about in the story. I'll copy maps for everyone tonight, and when you continue reading on your own tomorrow, you can plot the points of interest on your map."

As the week progressed, the students became interested in the focus areas in the story. Some students had even traveled to these places. So Mrs. Hilwiller suggested that they form research triads to share information beyond what the book provided. After composition of the triads was decided, she said, "Boys and girls, each time we plot a new story location, I'd like to invite the triads to research that area. For instance, if the character stops in New York, you could work on your own to investigate and log information about that city's people, geography, industry, culture, and so on. Then each day your group can get together to share what you've learned. Obviously, our book will provide some information, and you can check the library resources, too. Also, your parents may know something about the area. If you're on-line at home, maybe you could surf the net for more information or even locate someone from the area to interview.

"Please take your clipboards to your meetings each day so you can take notes from others in your group. Let's keep the map and all the data you collect in notebooks, so that after we finish the project, you'll be able to place the information into your portfolios if you wish. Oh, and don't forget, you may also include drawings and such. Some of you may even have some music from the area that you'd like to share with the rest of us."

The students had fun tracking the journey, and because of their research, they completed the book with far more understanding than if they had just read and discussed the story.

THINK-ALOUD SKIMMING

ACTIVITY: *Use think-alouds to develop technique of skimming informational text when doing research*
TEXT: *Articles on a chosen local, regional, national, or world issue, selected from newspapers, research journals, magazines focusing on multicultural themes (e.g., Faces, Rainbow, ZuZu, National Geographic World, Tapori), or downloaded from the Internet*
ASSESSMENT: *Using a checklist, note skimming techniques employed by each student*
MATERIALS: *Overhead projector and transparencies of articles*

"We've recently been focusing on poverty in our city," Mrs. Busch reviews with the class as the children settle into their favorite listening positions. "Many of you have been extending your research to take in poverty in other places across the world. Some of you have even brought in articles you've clipped from the newspaper or downloaded from the World Wide Web. So let's use these to broaden our investigation." Mrs. Busch then notices that Noelle is excitedly sharing something with LaTesha. "So", the teacher asks, "Noelle, did you have a good idea?"

"I was just telling LaTesha that there's a news special on homelessness on TV tonight. I could videotape it and bring it in for us to watch," responds Noelle.

"You've got a good point, Noelle," reinforces Mrs. Busch. "Television can help direct us toward interesting topics. But let's look into some other sources where we can seek information and learn how to use them.

"I've copied articles from some journals and have brought in some magazines from the library that we can use. Plus Mrs. Mussachio in the media center recommended that we investigate some Internet sources. She's even printed out a few articles for us, and she said that if you have time to visit after lunch, she'll be able to help you track down others.

"But," continues Mrs. Busch, "before you begin, I'd like to demonstrate the way skilled readers read magazines and newspapers when they're doing research. First, they skim through the text, reading the headings and subheadings. Then, they think about the article and decide whether they want to read it or move on to something that might be more pertinent. This is what I would like each of you to do after I finish a brief demonstration: skim, consider, decide."

At this point, Mrs. Busch moves to the overhead projector, where she has placed a copy of an article brought in by a student. She begins, "I'll share my thinking aloud with you, just as each of you will do in a few minutes in your research triads," and she then moves into the think-aloud. "Hmm. 'Hundreds Dead, Thousands Homeless in Ethiopia.' I wonder why. I wonder what happened there. Oh, the first subheading mentions the word 'drought.' There must have been a drought, where no rain fell for a long time, and that would mean crops would die. This next heading suggests that other countries are helping. I wonder what our country is doing. If I choose this article, I could probably get more information about this on the Internet—maybe even hook up with someone in Africa. Let's see—the next heading says 'More Drought Ahead.' My goodness, what are they going to do about that? Oh, here's a possible solution in the next heading, 'Relocation of Villages.' How awful! That means people will have to leave their homes. Oh, and this last heading suggests another issue, 'Climatologists Predict Changes.'"

Mrs. Busch goes on, "This sounds like an interesting article, and I may select it as my focus because I'd really like to know more about Africa. But also, I've already read some articles about the effects of climate change, so I could add onto knowledge that I already possess. Plus, I'm connected to the Internet at home and I could probably get some really detailed information there.

"OK, here's another article I thought I might just skim, 'New York City Homeless Find Refuge.' I don't really think I'm interested in this so much, because I already know a lot about it, and besides, I'd really like to investigate homelessness in another country. But maybe this article does connect to other countries, so I'll just skim through and see." Mrs. Busch quickly reads each heading aloud and continues, "I can see that it is focused only on New York, so I'm going to put it into the file tub." With that, she drops the article into a large plastic tub marked "To Be Filed."

Mrs. Busch then quickly models her focused skimming technique using one more article. At this point she decides which article is most interesting for her research and explains the reasoning behind that decision. After her oral explanation, she reaches for her journal and logs the article's bibliographic information and the reasons for her selection of that piece, sharing all of this with her student audience. Mrs. Busch knows that the journal will provide a solid segue into tomorrow's follow-up lesson, when she and the students move into the research process in greater depth.

At this point Mrs. Busch invites, "Skim through some articles and select a few that might be of interest. In about ten minutes, please gather your research triads together and take turns thinking aloud through the headings and subheadings of each article. You may discover that others in your triad have interesting articles that you would like to use, too. That's fine. The object right now is to complete the decision-making process using a think-aloud technique. If your group finishes before lunch, then go ahead and log your article's reference and the reasons for your selection in your journal, just as I did. I'll be meandering around with my checklist, logging the skimming techniques that I see each of you using."

The children then disperse around the classroom, while Mrs. Busch reaches for her clipboard with the checklist attached. Most students are anxious to choose a few articles and move into their triads, where they can use Mrs. Busch's think-aloud as a model. Their teacher and the reading teacher, who has just entered the room, offer assistance to students who are experiencing problems.

In the days that follow, Mrs. Busch notes that her demonstration has served as a scaffold for students as they move into more skilled reading behaviors and delve deeper into the research process.

SELLING AWARD-WINNING LITERATURE

ACTIVITY: *Use a "book sell" to encourage others to read a text, thereby broadening reading interests*
TEXT: *Text set of award-winning literature*
ASSESSMENT: *Collect group checklists logging attributes of each student's book-sell presentation*
MATERIALS: *Copies of book-sell checklist*

Early in the morning before the students arrived, Miss Nobel guided a cartful of books into the classroom. She had visited the library the day before, and with the help of the librarian, she had selected a variety of award-winning books that she planned to invite the students to read during sustained silent reading. Miss Nobel had noticed that many of her students were reading what she thought of as "junk." She decided that they could save their "junk reading" for home, just as she saved such reading for vacations, but during school, she felt the students should experience the works of highly skilled authors and illustrators. She had chosen thick books and thin books, easy books and difficult books, fiction and nonfiction, old books and new books. She hoped the collection had something for everyone.

That day when it was almost time for their half-hour period of sustained silent reading, Miss Nobel addressed the group regarding her intentions. "Boys and girls, I know that most of you have your own favorites that you're reading. That's great. We all have favorites. But sometimes we get so attached to one kind of book that we forget there are many wonderful books out there. I've gone to the library and collected a wide variety of highly acclaimed books. For the next month, I invite you to broaden your tastes and see if some award winners might also win your personal stamp of approval. After a couple of weeks, we'll start meeting in small groups and any member who has finished a good book can try to sell the others on it. By the end of the month, I hope that each of you will have had a chance to present at least one 'book sell.'"

Mohammed raised his hand to ask, "Miss Nobel, do we really have to read your books? I'm in the middle of a really good book that I want to finish."

"Mohammed, you can take that really good book home and finish it there, can't you?" responded his teacher.

"I guess so," answered Mohammed in a dejected voice.

"Obviously, most of you are in the middle of something good, and I apologize that your routine is being interrupted. But there's no perfect time for us to try this. Besides, these books may be even better than what you're reading. But we'll never know that unless we try them on for size," coaxed the teacher.

Throughout the month the students read the award winners. Some of them even found copies at home and brought them in for other class members. During the first two weeks, Miss Nobel asked the class to think about the commercials they saw on television, since the advertisers might use tactics they could adapt for their book sells. Then the children and Miss Nobel worked together to develop a list of attributes that a good book sell might encompass. Miss Nobel converted this into a checklist and copied it for each student. Then, each time a student shared a book sell, the rest of her group used the checklist to log the attributes she incorporated in her presentation.

When the groups passed the checklists on to Miss Nobel at the end of the month, she had a pretty good idea of what each student had done, even though she may not have seen much of a particular presentation. During the following month, Miss Nobel noticed that most of the students had indeed expanded their interests, and many were standing in line to read favorites that classmates had presented during book sells. As a matter of fact, many were still doing informal book sells!

INDEPENDENT ACTIVITIES WITH PRE- TO POSTREADING CONNECTIONS

> By definition children are pupils and learning is a human
> activity which least needs manipulation by others. Most
> learning is not the result of instruction. It is rather the result
> of unhampered participation in a meaningful setting.
>
> Ivan Illich

Although quiet classrooms are rapidly finding their way out of schools and into history books, there is certainly no reason to consider individual, independent work a thing of the past. There are actually many times when students should still be involved in individual endeavors. The difference is, however, that most of these individual endeavors eventually feed back into the group in some way. That is, they either become part of a larger collaborative project or they remain discrete but are shared with the group. This nurtures a sense of interconnectedness, belonging, and community spirit. How much more will students be able to contribute to society if they learn at a young age that what they do as individuals affects the whole, and that the whole is made better by each of the parts. This whole-parts interrelationship is called a holonomy. Within holonomic settings students learn to cooperate for group success, rather than to compete or to stand apart. Researchers working in the area of social aspects of education have provided considerable evidence that cooperative learning is more successful than competitive or individual learning. Furthermore, we hope that students experiencing this new paradigm of learning will find an inner satisfaction as they are involved in the diversity of a more community-spirited, multidisciplinary approach. Students in these learning communities come to know that diversity allows everyone to access, share, and celebrate his or her talents. Although each of the following activities is individual-centered, most often the independent work period is preceded or followed by some kind of community-centered activity.

There are also occasional periods, sometimes outside school hours, when students work together or with family members on some facet of their individual projects. Unlike the activities in the preceding chapters, those presented here span the phases of reading. Some of the most interesting, enticing, and rewarding activities are those that begin in prereading, extend across he reading act, and continue through postreading. A common pathway across the entire reading model not only helps rid the curriculum of the "a piece of this and a piece of that" mentality but also reinforces students' understandings of reading and text. Such connectedness weaves together the great variety of curricular pieces and binds the community. It ties individuals, partners, and small groups to the whole.

Prereading and postreading are symbiotic parts of a whole, as are individual students within a classroom community. It would be wonderful if all that we did in schools could connect and flow in such a way for, as the sages have told us, all learning is just making connections. The better the connections, the better the learning.

RESEARCH USING K-W-L

ACTIVITY: *Research a topic using the K-W-L technique (for a full description of this technique, see Donna Ogle's "K-W-L")*
TEXT: *Any text set (a collection of books related to a common topic) along with a variety of related print or audiovisual material*
ASSESSMENT: *Collect final drafts of K-W-L logs for each student's portfolio*
MATERIALS: *Writing tools*

The students in Mr. Young's class have begun a month-long thematic study called "Cultures: Celebrating Our Differences." The class decides that it might be fun for each student to study his or her own culture and then share it with the class. In the course of ensuing discussions it becomes clear that several students are studying the same culture; consequently some of them decide to work together, while others remain independent. Mr. Young invites the class to join him at the front of the room on the large area rug, so that they can decide how to start their research. Sarah shares, "I already know how I'm going to start because I want to tell about how my culture celebrates Yom Kippur."

"That's great!" responds Mr. Young. "And I'm sure that the rest of you know some things already about the culture you've selected. That's always a good place to start—with what you know. Actually, it's the beginning of a way of researching a topic that's called K-W-L. The three letters stand for what we *know*, what we *want* to know, and finally, what we've *learned*."

Mr. Young writes the key words on the chalkboard at the front of the room. He then moves to the chart taped to the wall and picks up an ink marker. "Now, for instance," he demonstrates, "if I wanted to study the Irish culture, I guess I'd begin by writing what I know about St. Patrick's Day." As he writes a few ideas on the chart, he goes on to say, "I could also write that I'm pretty sure that Ireland is northwest of Great Britain and that it's an island." He notes these points and then concludes, "When I'm researching later, I can verify this information. OK, now after you've written everything you know about your topic, why don't you share it with another student. Then perhaps as you share, you'll be reminded of other things you know; then you can add those things on, too."

The following day Mr. Young moves on to the "want to know" part of K-W-L, although some students have already tackled this independently. He explains, "Now, there must be some things you're wondering about your topic. For instance, for my topic, 'The Irish Culture,' I'm wondering how that whole thing about leprechauns got started. But I'd also like to know why potatoes are so important to Irish people." He notes these items on his growing list.

At this Cal interjects, "Yeah, but don't you wonder about all the fighting in Ireland that's always on the news?"

"Thanks. As a matter of fact, I do," agrees Mr. Young, as he writes this also. He notes a few more things he wonders about, and then invites, "Now, why don't you put some of your own wonders into writing and then later we'll share some together with the whole group. This may give us some more ideas."

After their period of brainstorming, the students are ready to search for answers to their questions in the materials Mr. Young and others have brought in to share. And what an assortment they've collected! Maria has brought in some postcards that her uncle sent from Italy. Nadia brought a treasured cookbook from Mexico, which she promised her mother she would guard with her life. Mr. Young ordered two films: one on Asia and one on Europe. He also rolled the encyclopedia cart down from Mrs. Steiner's room. Earlier that week, he had suggested that two students be responsible for collecting a list of all the topics, which was given to the librarian, who gathered related reading from the shelves. Barry's mother was kind enough to make a trip to the public library with the list and returned with a collection of books. Zita and her father stopped by the automobile association and collected a few brochures on some European countries.

As the students and Mr. Young research, they find answers to their questions along with much more. It is often difficult for students to stop working long enough to share new and exciting pieces of information with friends. Because of the wealth of information, Mr. Young suggests that everyone focus on one particular facet of their selected culture that could be shared in some way with the class. He provides a model for this when he announces, "Ireland is a large, broad topic. I've become very interested in the potato famine, so I'm going to develop a piece of writing about it that I can later share with all of you. Why don't you decide on some aspect of your topic that you'd like to share with the class? I'm not certain yet if I'll use transparencies or maps or maybe I'll write a short drama. If I write the drama, I'll need some actors to help me. Think about how you'll present your topic, too."

At the end of the unit, Nadia brings in some Mexican food to share while she presents information concerning the festival at which the food might be eaten. Ling brings in a collection of artifacts from her Chinese culture, and explains each one. Tom, who had selected the Native American culture, shares a videotaped interview he had conducted with a member of the Tuscarora tribe.

It was quite a culmination as students celebrated the culture of their choice through their own particular interpretational vehicle.

Afterwards, Mr. Young asked the students to develop final drafts highlighting what they'd learned, to be included in their portfolios along with the K and W logs.

ACTIVITY: *Conduct research using a variety of sources from both in and out of school as background for a panel discussion*
TEXT: *David Burnie, Tree*
ASSESSMENT: *Collect final projects for portfolios*
MATERIALS: *Text sets and a variety of related material*

Later that year Mr. Young's class is immersed in a thematic unit involving the study of living things. Students are invited to select a research topic that they feel is of utmost importance for the maintenance of our planet and relates to air, water, plant life, or animal life. Mr. Young advises, "Think about your topics for a while first, because later we'll have panel discussions, at which point you'll be able to take a stand. This will help when you eventually compose letters to politicians, newspaper editors, or companies that disagree with your point of view. That is, the panel discussions will help provide food for thought."

He then reminds the students what they learned concerning the K-W-L method and suggests it would be helpful to begin by writing everything they know about their chosen topic. He checks to see if everyone is set to begin, and soon the room is a flurry of activity. While Mr. Young is working with some students in another part of the room, Chrystal and Kyla look through the literature (newspaper and magazine articles, books, pamphlets from the government and from ecology organizations, etc.) that the teacher, students, and parents have collected. The two girls decide on the same topic: recycling. Although they will work independently on their research, they decide to meet occasionally to discuss progress.

The following day Mr. Young begins a read-aloud using the book *Tree*, inviting the students to connect the text to their own topics. After the teacher has read two pages, Kyla says that she has begun thinking about ways families can recycle to help cut down on deforestation. Amal tells Kyla that Mr. Oniso, the owner of the local arboretum, is very interested in this topic, and that maybe he would be a resource. Chrystal is excited about this possibility, too.

Over the next few days, the students spend time both in and out of school researching their topics. Kyla and Chrystal use the telephone in the school office to call Mr. Oniso, who invites them to stop by some evening. Kyla's father drives the girls, and they are happy to discover that Mr. Oniso has a passionate interest in deforestation and is anxious to share his own knowledge as well as some literature that he has collected. Fascinated by his dedication and expertise, the girls ask if he'd be interested in speaking to their class some time. The next day, when the girls share this possibility with Mr. Young, he suggests that they check the calendar and then write a letter of invitation to Mr. Oniso. The girls dive into the letter and their project with extra zeal.

After weeks of background building, the students feel they're ready to take a stand. The class divides into four panels: air, water, plant life, and animal life. Mr. Young asks each panel to select several key issues to present and to hand in a list of these along with a description of each student's responsibilities on the panel. Because he knows a model may be needed for the discussions, he plans to show video footage of a similar panel presentation with rebuttals.

DIALOGUE JOURNALS

ACTIVITY: *Write ongoing responses to text in dialogue journal for written replies by a partner*
TEXT: *Charlie and the Chocolate Factory, James and the Giant Peach, Charlie and the Great Glass Elevator, The Enormous Alligator (a Roald Dahl author text set)*
ASSESSMENT: *Collect journals to assess and log data regarding comprehension of story*
MATERIALS: *Literary journals (bought or made), writing tools*

To introduce a new literature activity, Miss Donnelly explained that each person would choose to be in one of four

Roald Dahl literature groups. She then shared a bit of background on Dahl, but said that she would be introducing the author even more when she read aloud one of his shorter books, *The Enormous Alligator*. This would give everyone an initial taste of Dahl's wonderful imagination. Then, as they enjoyed this text together, she would demonstrate an activity that the students would be invited to do with a friend.

That first day, Miss Donnelly read about half the book, with the students discussing along the way. She then mentioned they'd soon be finding a spot in the room where they could write.

"Can we write together?" asked Mario.

"You'll be able to sit together for this activity, but it *is* a quiet, thinking time, so you'll not be writing together," responded Miss Donnelly. She then taped a large piece of paper to the wall and reached for her black marker as she continued, "Sometimes it's fun to respond to a text in writing—to put your thoughts concerning the story, the author, or his writing down on paper. But it's even more fun to write when you know a friend will be reading what you've written, agreeing with it, disagreeing with it, adding to it, or commenting in some way in response to what you wrote. So that's what we're going to do, but the responder will reply in writing, right below your own writing. In other words, your journal will become a written dialogue. For this reason, we'll call these 'dialogue journals.' Let me show you," she said, as she turned to the blank paper and wrote her think-aloud. "Roald Dahl has such a preposterous imagination. I wonder how he thinks up some of the things he does. I once saw *Charlie and the Chocolate Factory* on videotape and so many wild things happened. But I guess that is what I enjoy about his stories. He can take an ordinary world and turn it C-R-A-Z-Y! This book is somewhat different, though, because he chooses to use an alligator as one of the main characters, and he didn't use animals in *Charlie*."

Here Miss Donnelly turned to the class and invited them to put their own thought concerning the first half of *The Enormous Alligator* down on paper. Then everyone, including Miss Donnelly, swapped papers with a friend so the friend could respond. Later, when Miss Donnelly collected the papers to evaluate the activity, she noticed that most students had followed her lead and written a general critique of the author. To encourage more creative thinking, she decided that as she finished the read-aloud with them, she would demonstrate other ways in which they might respond to the story. They might share what they liked or didn't like, write what they wondered about, predict what might happen, or describe anything else that caught their attention. Then, she'd also show how they could focus on the craft of writing: the words Dahl chose to use, his sentence structure, the lead-ins he used, or any other facet of the way he crafted his writing.

In the days that followed, it was easy for the students to see their options because Miss Donnelly joined a group, read what they read, wrote about it, and dialogued herself with a partner. She could always rely on her own work to use as a model for students who got stuck in one groove or who didn't understand the activity. Miss Donnelly was an integral part of the class literacy community.

SEEING THROUGH THE EYES OF CHARACTER

ACTIVITY: *Write in journal from the point of view of a story character, then use these entries as an impetus for small group discussions*
TEXT: *Patricia Reilly Giff, Purple Climbing Days; Judy Blume, Tales of a Fourth Grade Nothing*
ASSESSMENT: *Collect journals to assess comprehension of and "feel" for character; gather oral reading data for a few students*
MATERIALS: *Literary journals (bought or made), pencils, puppets, hats*

Mrs. Fronczek reminds the class of a Patricia Reilly Giff book that they read two months earlier. Immediately the students start remembering the characters they liked: "I liked Emily Arrow—remember her?" asks Camisha. "I liked Beast the best. He was cool!" adds Denny. "Well, Patricia Reilly Giff certainly does know how to create a memorable character!" Mrs. Fronczek responds. "As a matter of fact, we're going to do something with those unique characters. To begin, I'd like you to get your copies of *Purple Climbing Days* and work in groups to develop a list of characters. Then each person in each group can pick a character, and as you read, you can pretend to be that character. In other words, just put yourself in his or her shoes. Try to think just like your character thinks, feel like the character feels, become that character in your mind. I'm going to post a list of character traits, because it may help you to ask yourself, 'Is this character sad? Kind? Helpful? Generous? Mean? Stubborn?' Let's practice a bit."

Mrs. Fronczek then reads the first chapter aloud, stopping at points she had marked earlier. The first couple of times she grabs a puppet and uses it to voice her character's thoughts. For the next two points she dons a hat from the class's collection and transforms herself into her character. She then goes on reading, inviting students to share their remarks concerning their own characters each time she stops. Students step up to the front and put on hats or grab puppets, which serve as an impetus for transformation into a story character.

At the end of the chapter, Mrs. Fronczek passes out the students' literary journals and invites everyone to move to a comfortable area and respond by writing, instead of talking, in the voice of their character. "Don't forget to keep the list of character traits in mind," she reminds.

"I can't hear my character," whines Jessie. The teacher hands this unhappy student a puppet and tells him to write down what his character has to say about the situation. When the student still has trouble, Mrs. Fronczek slips another puppet onto her own hand and says to Jessie's puppet, "Hi! I'm Richard and I hate gym. Boy, do I hate gym. Do you like gym? I know most of the kids do, but I don't. I hope you don't either, do you?"

Jessie giggles and has his puppet respond, "I like gym."

"Good," encourages Mrs. Fronczek. "Now, just write that down in your journal."

When everyone seems involved, the teacher calls some students aside to have them read aloud from the text so she can log reading behavior for an oral reading analysis. She wants to see if these students are using optimal strategies to get through print, and this seems a good chance to catch them alone while allowing them to remain involved with the book. Each oral reading takes but a few minutes.

Later, when the students have finished writing, their teacher suggests, "When your groups meet to discuss the chapter, why don't you first invite each member to read his or her entry. Then after all the entries are read, perhaps you'll have something to say related to the characters and the way they act." Mrs. Fronczek then designates the meeting area for each group, inviting students to sit in circles so they can meet the eyes of other contributors as they discuss the story.

CONSTRUCTING FAIRY TALES FROM WEB STRUCTURES

ACTIVITY: *Insert story elements from a fairy tale in a narrative web; later use web structure to develop original fairy tale*
TEXT: *Hans Christian Andersen, The Ugly Duckling; fairy tale text set with audio tapes*
ASSESSMENT: *Collect original fairy tales (with drafts) for portfolios, along with some student-selected webs*
MATERIALS: *Large chart paper or chalkboard, paper, writing tools*

"Many of you have heard the story 'The Ugly Duckling,' or perhaps you've seen it on TV?" Several children raise their hands as Mrs. Bening looks up with questioning eyes. "My mom just read that story to me!" responds Enrique.

"Great! I'm glad some of you are acquainted with the story because we're going to be sharing it now—and I think that reading a book over again is just like getting to have dessert twice!" Everyone laughs. "Before we begin this story, however, I'd like each of you to notice this chart. It has spots for many parts of a story. A fairy tale has parts that are especially easy to put into these spots. So, as I read, you be thinking about who the characters are, what the setting is, what some of the major events are, and what the ending is like. In fact, why don't we make a guess at some of these before we even begin. Some of you who have heard it before will have pretty good guesses, I'd bet," Mrs. Bening encourages.

The children make a few guesses about the setting. Most of them agree that the Ugly Duckling is probably a main character. Some remember aloud some of the events, which are also filled in.

Then, as Mrs. Bening takes the chart down so as not to detract from the emotive experience of the story, she invites, "Please just sit back and relax now while I read. Then later we'll decide on the other elements in the story that we want to add—or maybe revise." When Mrs. Bening finishes *The Ugly Duckling* the children work together to reconstruct the story framework on the chart, discussing and sometimes

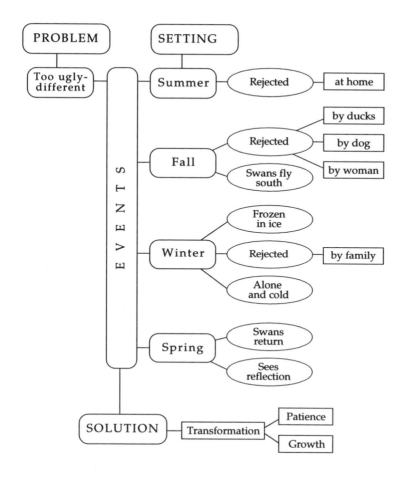

A complete web for "The Ugly Duckling"

disagreeing as they progress. After they've finished, Mrs. Bening suggests that this kind of activity is helpful because "our brains like to have ideas arranged in a logical order. As a matter of fact, our brains like to use that same organization in order to create and write, too." She then invites, "I've put on the back shelf a variety of fairy tales that you've brought in and I've collected. I'd like each of you to find one that you'd like to read. If you have trouble with it, perhaps I have it on tape and then you can follow along. Anyway, after you finish, would you please come up with one of these story frameworks to think about your story? They won't look exactly alike in their form—even for the same story—so you develop yours the way you think it should be. Then we'll share and compare."

After the students have had experience creating story webs and have shared them, their teacher tells them that these webs can be wonderful "holders" for their own stories. She explains, "Each of you can put your own invented, original setting in the setting spots, your own characters into the character spots, and so on. If you want to, you may work with a co-author; it's up to you. Think about it as a possible activity for writer's workshop tomorrow. Also, if you feel that one of your webs is really good, you may want to put it in your portfolio."

FINDING POEMS

ACTIVITY: *Search for ways a topic can be interpreted through poetry*
TEXT: *Poetry text set and Ann Durell and Marilyn Sachs, The Big Book for Peace*
ASSESSMENT: *Videotape students' oral sharing of poetry; review tapes to log student presentation strengths*
MATERIALS: *Writing tools*

Miss Miles wanted to expose her students to more poetry, so she decided that since they were involved with a thematic unit called "Peace," it might be interesting to see all the different ways that they, as well as poets, interpreted peace through poetry. "Last night Manuel and Sarita stayed to help me gather together all of our poetry books and to borrow some from the library and from Mr. Miller's classroom. We have quite a collection!" begins Miss Miles. "I thought it might be fun to see how poets interpret the idea of peace. I actually found a whole bunch of 'peace poems' in *The Big Book for Peace*. Let me share a few." So the students relax together on the rug in the corner of the room to celebrate poetry as it is read aloud.

Afterwards the students dig right into the stack of anthologies and poetry collections to locate some of their favorites, such as *Old Turtle*, *The Great Peace March*, and *Brother Eagle, Sister Sky*. As they are perusing the pile, their teacher asks what they would like to do with the peace poems they find.

Because they are just beginning, they are unsure of what they might like to do. Miss Miles suggests that maybe, for each poem they select, they could log its title, the name of the book it came from, and the page number for reference. Then later they can decide what they will do with the collection.

Suddenly Cynthia jumps up and exclaims, "I just *love* this poem! Don't you, Miss Miles?"

"Yes, I do," responds Miss Miles, "and Cynthia, if you'd like to write it down to save or put it up on a large chart for all of us to savor, please do."

"Can I do that, too, Miss Miles?" implores Andre.

"Certainly, that would be wonderful—"

Just then, from a different part of the room, Manuel inquires, "What about this, Miss Miles? This is that book by Raffi, *Like Me and You*, but it's also a song, and so can't it be a poem, too? It's about how everyone in the world is connected—that's the beginning of peace, isn't it?"

"Sounds logical to me, Manuel. But why not check with some of the others in the room. Their opinion is as important as mine," responds the teacher.

"Can we do pictures for the poems, too, just like Jack Prelutsky?" interjects Andre, who is now preparing to copy his poem.

"Sure!" answers the teacher. "It looks like we're deciding what we'll do after all!"

Everyone, including Miss Miles, continues to search. After about 45 minutes, she calls the group together so that everyone can share a favorite poem and the group can talk about how each relates to the central topic. She has already set up the video camera on a tripod. She invites Sal to press the "On" and "Off" buttons to record each presentation.

Over the next few days, the class continues to find and present additional poems. Later that week many students begin writing some "peace poems" of their own. Eventually Nancy says that some of them would like to develop a class anthology on peace.

As everyone begins to play off Nancy's idea, Miss Miles interjects, "Well, do you know what I think we should do?"

"What?" her listeners ask in unison.

"I think we should bundle all of your poems into a text and send it to a publisher!"

. . . .

IN CELEBRATION OF

INTERDISCIPLINARY

RESPONSE

The most common medium we use is language. One feature of a medium is that it mediates and anything that mediates changes what it conveys; the map is not the territory and the text is not the event. We learn to write and to draw, to dance and to sing, in order to re-present the world as we know it.

Elliot W. Eisner

In 1967, Joni Mitchell first shared "Both Sides Now" through her music. Then, in 1992, Alan Baker shared his interpretation of that text through beautiful illustrations in a book of the same name. Could someone develop artistic movement for these words? Of course, and many did on the dance floors of the late 1960s. Could another interpret this work through film? Obviously. There are as many modes of interpretation as there are sign systems, and there are as many interpretations as there are star systems. Isn't it wonderful that we are all different and that we see, interpret, and create in a variety of ways?

For so many years, we educators treated literature as though its meaning were normative, that it had but one "correct" interpretation to which, of course, the teacher held the key. Now we realize that we all view through unique lenses—sometimes slightly different and sometimes very different. As we construct meaning through our own particular lens, we also seek complementary channels for interpretation. The one-right-answer comprehension dittos and the extrinsic rewards of programmed instruction are being banished from today's classrooms. Gone, too, are the days when each discipline was treated as a distinct entity, when talk of science didn't enter a history lesson or mathematics a music period.

In celebration of their individuality, we offer students a wide menu from which to select an avenue for interpreting text; similarly, we offer them numerous texts to help develop their knowledge of other subject areas. When students reinterpret meaning from one channel through another (a process called "transmediation"), they construct something quite special and, we hope, are then able to share this construction. It is through these interpretations and reinterpretations that we enrich our communities. How very boring life would be without music, dance, numeracy, architecture, and so many other modes of communication. When we offer students a variety of opportunities, we lay the groundwork for future creators of all sorts. Teachers need only extend invitations, respond to students' needs, and celebrate their products. The options are endless.

USING THE SCIENTIFIC METHOD

ACTIVITY: *Dig in soil to search for interesting objects/artifacts and hypothesize as to their source*
TEXT: *Norma Gentner, Dig a Dinosaur; David Macaulay, Motel of Mysteries*
ASSESSMENT: *Place group chart (labeled "Group Scribe") into scribe's portfolio*
MATERIALS: *Child's plastic wading pool filled with soil from a field or forest, magnifying glasses, chart paper, ink marker*

In the course of a unit on dinosaurs, Mrs. Grieco invited one group of her kindergarten students to a shared book experience using *Dig a Dinosaur*. The text is also a song, and the children had already enjoyed listening to an audiotaped version; this supported them as they read. Two days later, Mrs. Grieco and the group are singing their way through the book one more time. The teacher notices that a few students are still making the digging motions called for in the text, so she asks, "Who would like to do what real scientists do and go on a dig?"

All the children respond with an excited "Yeah!" knowing that it must have something to do with the wading pool full of dirt sitting at the back of their room. They also have another clue: the day before, Mrs. Grieco asked them to bring in their sand shovels. Their excited faces clearly demonstrate the conclusions they have drawn.

Their teacher quickly reviews the ways in which scientists discover through gathering data ("digging"), making hypotheses ("guessing"), and analyzing ("finding out if you've guessed right"). She then proposes they dig for interesting objects in the wading pool. "I collected the soil from a wooded area near my house. There are lots of birds and small animals there, but a lot of people also use the woods for hiking and picnics. Let's make a list of some of the things that we might find in the pool or that might happen," she says, and she gives Sonya a marker so she can act as the group's scribe. Mrs. Grieco goes to work with another group, but returns to read the chart with the digging group. Then, after she gives them a brief reminder about sharing materials, the children move to the wading pool where they begin digging and observing. Mrs. Grieco suggests that Tai take the tape recorder to the "dig" and play the *Dig a Dinosaur* tape softly while the children act as scientists.

A few minutes later Mrs. Grieco looks up from another group to see BettyLou holding a small object and exclaiming, "Look what I found! It looks like an animal bone." With that, the children in the group move closer and begin to analyze BettyLou's find, while Mrs. Grieco continues with her group.

TEXT, MUSIC, AND MOVEMENT

ACTIVITY: *Select parts of a shared text to interpret through movement*
TEXT: *Byrd Baylor, I'm in Charge of Celebrations*
ASSESSMENT: *Make anecdotal notes on students' group participation*
MATERIALS: *Recorded music and player*

Ms. Eyer's class has just finished reading *I'm in Charge of Celebrations* by Byrd Baylor, who often writes in a poetic, rhythmic, and sensual style. This is a text that the teacher thinks has strong possibilities for interpretation through movement, so she says to the class, "We've talked about the rhythm of this text, the way it feels like poetry—even looks like poetry. Let's think about this part." The teacher begins reading a section that describes things that are worth a celebration, times when "your heart will pound...and you'll catch your breath like you were breathing some new kind of air."

After reading the passage, Ms. Eyer says, "Now, when I think about the word 'celebration,' I want to throw my hands into the air and twirl. Then when I get to the part about the pounding heart, it seems like maybe I should place one hand near my heart, but at the end where it says 'catch your breath like you were breathing some new kind of air,' I feel that I should be more or less relaxing my body and looking up holding my palms outward. Does anyone want to try my interpretation with me?"

Two students are interested, so Ms. Eyer suggests, "When I say 'one,' we'll slowly move our hands above our heads and twirl. Then when I say 'two,' we'll gradually move one hand down to our hearts, and at 'three' we'll look upward, stop moving, relax, and really exaggerate breathing in while we hold our palms out. All set?"

With the help of teachers Gail Nye and Sharon Miles, students from Maplemere Elementary School enjoy performing in a musical adaptation of "The Castaways"

And they begin, the whole thing a model for what each small group will be invited to do. Ms. Eyer feels that it is very important that this not be a polished performance so that students will not feel intimidated about attempting their own interpretations. To help support the movement with tempo, she puts Vivaldi's "The Four Seasons" into the CD player.

When the groups meet, she moves to each one in turn, asking if any member takes dance lessons and inviting that person to take the lead, using his or her expertise to help the group interpret. After the groups have had time to work through some movements, Ms. Eyer asks, "Does anyone want to demonstrate a movement while someone else in the group reads?" Three students raise their hands, so the class sits back to enjoy this unique performance of text.

UNDERGIRDING TEXT WITH SONG

ACTIVITY: *Enhance decoding skills (beginning readers) or understanding of content (skilled readers) by reading text founded upon the rhythm, rhyme, and melody of a song*
TEXT: *Raffi, Down by the Bay (book and audiotape); audiotape or CD of a song from a musical, along with text copied from the jacket*
ASSESSMENT: *After shared reading experience, observe and log individual reading behaviors*
MATERIALS: *Tape recorder*

As the children skipped into Mr. Covel's class they could hear the familiar voice of Raffi wafting through the air. It was exciting to watch the expression on each face as the students entered the room. Soon many of the boys and girls were singing along to "Down by the bay, where the watermelons grow...."

Later in the morning Mr. Covel said, "I noticed that many of you liked Raffi's 'Down by the Bay.' What did you like about it?"

"It just makes me happy," smiled Lucy-anne.

"Because it rhymes!" added Marguerite.

"Because it's kind of goofy," laughed Greg.

"Well, I like it because it's Raffi!" affirmed Antonina.

"But," said Mr. Covel, "did you know that there's a book for that song? Look," he said as he lifted the book up for all to see.

"Read it! Read it, Mr. Covel! Read it!" they all shouted.

As Mr. Covel sang his way through the book, many children joined in. By the end, most knew much of the sequence. "Sing it with me," invited Mr. Covel, and the children sang their way through.

"Let's use the tape," suggested Bill.

"Good idea," complimented Mr. Covel, and he asked Isabella to put the tape in the recorder and turn it on.

The students celebrated their way through the song again and again that day and in the days that followed. Mr. Covel observed, collecting detailed information on the students who were adequately pointing to the words in the printed text as they sang along. Then later in the week, Daryl created a new line: "Did you ever see a squirrel, wearing a curl, down by the bay?" It wasn't long before the others began to make up their own rhymes following the song's pattern. Mr. Covel scribed each child's original onto a large page with room for an illustration. After the children finished drawing, their teacher collated their pictures into a book that they could take turns taking home to share. Parents were quick to respond, expressing how delighted they were to see their own child's contributions as well as his or her growing competence in print.

Seeing the excitement that book had generated, Mr. Covel purchased a few more Raffi books along with another tape as an invitation to further enjoyment.

THROUGH THE LENS OF THE ARTIST

ACTIVITY: *Create a mural, beginning during prereading and adding details as information is gathered from text*
TEXT: *Helen Cowcher, Rainforest and Antarctica (both levels)*
ASSESSMENT: *After rehearsal, record mural on each child's videotape while the student describes the parts she played in bringing the whole to fruition, or photograph mural and ask student to provide a caption*
MATERIALS: *Long sheets of newsprint (ends of rolls from local newspaper publisher) or butcher paper, construction paper, paint and*

brushes, small cups, paper towels, scissors, pencils, glue, tape recorder and audiotape, video camera and videotape

The students in Miss Odien and Miss Hoffman's room had just begun a focused study of ecological issues. After discussion, the class members decided that they'd begin their journey with an investigation of ways in which the planet is changing. They had already begun collecting articles from newspapers and magazines. Because Miss Odien was very involved with environmental concerns, she had been collecting books, articles, magazines, brochures, and other printed matter for several years, so the class ecology text set was large and comprehensive.

"We have two great books for our literature studies this week," announced Miss Hoffman. "Most of you have already selected the group you want to join, and you know which book that group will be reading. But whether you're reading *Antarctica* or *Rainforest*, you'll be involved in the creation of a mural." "Can we use the display boards, Miss Hoffman?" asked Michael excitedly.

"Sure! And some of you might come up with an alternative plan," she responded.

Miss Odien listed the art materials available (colored paper, glue, scissors, and so forth) and discussed some first steps. "If you make a list of your mural's animals, trees, clouds, and other things, then you can each choose something to be responsible for. But it may not be wise to paste them onto the mural until you have everyone's contributions," recommended Miss Odien.

Then Miss Hoffman added, "Please feel free to use any of the references in the room that you may need to settle arguments or to locate new information. Miss Odien and I thought that creating the mural would really get us in the mood for the reading we'll be doing. As we read the books we'll be able to add more items, so that each mural will show what you discovered by reading."

During the week as Miss Odien worked with one group, the other spent time working on the mural. The *Rainforest* group set up the tape recorder in their corner so they could listen to *Tropical Jungle*, an audiotape of sounds from the jungle, which, they said, would help them get even more in the mood. The two murals grew rich with information as the students collected new ideas from their literature study texts as well as from the other reference sources in the room.

When the murals were finished, Miss Odien asked the groups to brainstorm some ways in which they might be used. The *Rainforest* group decided to place theirs in the hall with several posters to encourage ecological awareness. They also decided to send for information on environmental groups and display it by their mural, so passers-by might be enticed to join.

The *Antarctica* group decided to use their mural as a backdrop for a dramatic performance that they had already begun to script. Lilly inspired the others to create a videotape of their performance. They hoped that they would be able to copy the tape and send it off to Lilly's cousin, whose class shared the group's interest in making the world a better place.

Leigh-Ann Hildreth's students at Maplemere Elementary School dramatize their adapted version of the Great Kapoc Tree

SUMMARY PICTURES

ACTIVITY: *Take turns creating illustrations for book chapters as they are read aloud and collaborate on a caption for each illustration*

TEXT: *Rebecca Caudill, Did You Carry the Flag Today, Charlie?;
Cynthia Rylant, Missing May*
ASSESSMENT: *Copy and place each child's contribution in his working
portfolio*
MATERIALS: *White paper, pencils, crayons, two pieces of tagboard for
booklet cover, stapler*

Mr. Cooper shares the cover of the new text he will use for a
read-aloud and asks the students what they think the book
will be about. "You know, class, illustrators are really good
at interpreting text. Pictures can really enhance a book, but
not all books have pictures. This book has only a few, so I
thought it might be fun for us to create our own picture for
each chapter. Just before we start each read-aloud, someone
will be selected to draw for that day. How many of you
would like to listen and draw?" asks Mr. Cooper. Numerous
hands shoot into the air. "OK, let's start with Nina. Nina, just
get a piece of white paper and turn up enough at the bottom
so that there will be a place to add a summary sentence when
the chapter is finished. Also, you may want to just listen for
the first page or so to capture the setting in your mind's eye."
As everyone listens and discusses, Nina draws. When the
chapter is finished, Nina shares her illustration with the
others, who celebrate her wonderful interpretation of a small
house with a small family amid a montage of mountains.

"Let's think of a good sentence for this chapter that we can
write under the picture," suggests Mr. Cooper. After the
sentence is decided upon and written, Nina selects the person who will draw the next day during the read-aloud. But
she also adds, "I need to work on my picture just a little more
before I put it in the 'save' pile."

Throughout the year, the students enjoy reminiscing
about the book through their captioned pictures that have
now been stapled together into a booklet with a cover added.
Of course, each student always turns to her own page
first—just to make sure it's still there.

COMPARING VERSIONS OF FAIRY TALES

ACTIVITY: *Develop a class version of "Little Red Riding Hood" and
compare it with other versions of the tale*

TEXT: *Ed Young, Lon Po Po*
ASSESSMENT: *List fairy tale elements discussed in the course of developing class composition and use this as a basis for a checklist to assess transfer of learning evidenced through individual performance*
MATERIALS: *Overhead projector and transparency (or large chart paper), marker, large squares of butcher or construction paper, pencils, watercolors*

"Everyone find a partner," invites Ms. Rao, "and then sit eye-to-eye and knee-to-knee as you and your partner together create your version of 'Little Red Riding Hood.' Remember how the visiting storyteller entertained us with her story about Achilles, and remember how you liked Tomie dePaola's *Strega Nona*? It should be fun to put two heads together and reconstruct 'Little Red Riding Hood.' Later we'll use some of your ideas to develop a class story."

"Should we write ours down, Ms. Rao?" asks Kerstin.

"We will be writing later, but right now, let's just get ready for the writing by reconstructing the story out loud," Ms. Rao answers. "Is there anyone who doesn't know the story?" she adds. Enid raises her hand, so Ms. Rao invites Greta, a capable friend of Enid's, to share with her. Both girls look pleased.

Ms. Rao weaves her way among the children, enjoying the versions and logging an occasional note in her records. Eventually, she tells the class that it is time to bring the tales to a close so that they can create as a large group. Then she explains, "Please join me up here by the overhead projector so that you can dictate the story. I'll be your scribe and write it down for you. Who would like to begin?"

"Once upon a time...," suggests Juan at the same time that Bert says, "Once there was...."

"OK," responds Ms. Rao, "which will it be?"

"Almost all fairy tales start with 'Once upon a time,' and I like the way that sounds. Can't we use it?" asks Juan.

Most indicate that they agree and Bert doesn't disagree, so Ms. Rao asks the group to help her spell as she writes what Juan dictates. They continue in this manner, sometimes squeezing revisions in and sometimes crossing out lines, so that by the end of the story, the overhead has become a good example of a typical rough draft. Ms. Rao then suggests, "How about if I transfer this onto some pages so that you can illustrate each one. Let's think about where we want the page breaks."

Later the students illustrate in pencil and then watercolor what Ms. Rao has copied for them. Mrs. Mosandl, a senior citizen who helps out in the class on Tuesdays, traces over their pencil lines with a black marker and then adds a title page and front and back covers. Ms. Rao later binds the pages using the heavy-duty stapler. The students can now borrow their special class book to share at home with their parents.

While the children were working on their illustrations, Ms. Rao began reading *Lon Po Po*, a fairy tale from the Chinese tradition, welcoming comparisons to Western tales along the way.

"Look," exclaims Umberto, "Ed Young's story and ours both begin with 'Once.'"

"Somebody leaves in both stories," suggests Elizabeth, "but in his story it's the mother and in ours it's the little girl."

"Just like we noticed in those other fairy tales, the number three—three girls!" Teddy shouts as if he's discovered gold.

And the children continue finding similarities. After a while, Ms. Rao suggests that they all bring in anything that might be related to a fairy tale. "I have a very old version of 'Red Riding Hood' by the Brothers Grimm that I'd like to share with all of you. But you may bring other items—besides books, that is." It is amazing what has accumulated by the end of the week: a whole library of fairy tale books (which they enjoy during sustained silent reading time), and also a fairy tale cup, night light, toothbrush, cookie cutter, pajamas, watch, and a raft of other things that each donor is very proud to share.

COLLECTING, TABULATING, AND COMPARING DATA

ACTIVITY: *To inform the public, collect, analyze, and interpret data on quantity of red meat, poultry, fish, and meatless meals consumed and similar data from restaurant menus*
TEXT: *Menus from local restaurants*
ASSESSMENT: *Develop a checklist with which to respond to each student log; add student-constructed graphs and charts to portfolios*
MATERIALS: *Chart-size quadrille paper or teacher-constructed large graph paper, markers*

Students in Mrs. Bream's class were involved in inquiries related to health and nutrition. An earlier unit had revealed that most rainforests have been destroyed to make room for cattle pastures. Now, as the class began to discuss nutrition, they considered diets that did not rely on red meat. It was at that point that Mrs. Bream hypothesized, "I bet fewer people are eating red meat now. I know when I go to restaurants with friends, many of us order chicken or seafood. What about your families? Do you have red meat every night?"

Students began discussing their own family menus and what they enjoyed eating. Eventually, Joel said, "Why don't we keep track of what we all eat and then compare?"

"Great," responded Mrs. Bream, "let's. I'll make a chart while you're at lunch and when you return we'll begin with what everyone just ate. But then, what will we do with all the data we collect?"

"Well, we could add it all up and see how much more of one thing we had," suggested Batik.

"We could also check into the prices and see what costs the most to eat," added Andrina, the class economist.

"What do the rest of you think? Any other ideas?" Mrs. Bream hesitated, and then went on, "Well, keep thinking during lunch, and when you come back we'll begin our research."

When the students returned and began logging their lunch foods on the chart she had constructed, Mrs. Bream suggested, "I had an idea for another thing we could do. Maybe we could collect menus from all the restaurants around here and see how many meat entrées they list."

"What's an entrée?" asked Robbie.

"That's the main part of the meal and it's often built around meat, like fried chicken or fillet of sole or spaghetti—"

"Or hamburgers! Mmmm," drooled Patricia.

"Patricia! You just ate!" teased Mrs. Bream. "Anyway, yes, hamburgers could be an entrée, but usually they're listed as sandwiches because they're a small meal. Well, I guess quarter-pounders aren't!"

Having noticed that the students were not very menu literate, Mrs. Bream became even more enthused with her initial idea. She went on, "OK, so what do you think? After we investigate a little about this new genre called menus, we can start gathering some data from them. I even bet the whole community would be interested in our results. Maybe we could send a little article to the newspaper."

"My uncle works at the Red Lobster restaurant. I could ask him for a menu," Rosha volunteered.

"Yeah, and we're supposed to go out tonight for my dad's birthday. I'll try to get a menu from the restaurant," Zach added.

"Does McDonald's have a menu we can take out or should I copy theirs from the wall?" asked Ginny. When no one seemed to know, she continued, "I know. I'll just ask them and see."

"Sounds like we're off and running—as usual," said Mrs. Bream with a tinge of pride. She always enjoyed being an active part of the group herself, and this class kept getting more and more exciting. "Be thinking about who might like to know about the results we come up with. And also let everyone know if you come up with any other ideas besides comparing the amounts consumed and their costs. Oh, and please keep a log of your endeavors."

INTERPRETING MYTHS THROUGH MULTIPLE INTELLIGENCES

ACTIVITY: *Experience myths through a variety of literature and develop a plan to interpret and present favorites*
TEXT: *Ingri D'Aulaire and Edgar D'Aulaire, Greek Myths; Frieda Gates and Yoshi Miyake, Owl Eyes; Henry Gilford, The Reader's Theater Mythology Plays; William F. Russell, Classic Myths to Read Aloud; Ludmila Zeman, Gilgamesh the King; or any mythology text set*
ASSESSMENT: *Students develop a tool or description of the avenue through which their final presentation will be assessed*
MATERIALS: *Films, newspapers, and magazines referring to myths*

As Miss Ceprano and Mr. Kieffer's class entered their room, the students' eyes were drawn to the easel placed strategically at the entryway. A new quote shouted its message from one of Miss Ceprano's attractive posters: "Those who cannot learn from the past may be condemned to repeat it."

"Ah! That's easy!" boasted Elaine. "My five-year-old brother just learned all about that. He left his old football on the front lawn and it was gone in the morning. Then he got a new one for his birthday and he forgot it again when he was playing in the neighbor's yard. Now it's gone, too. He was so upset. We all felt really awful, but my mom said that's how we all learn—by our mistakes."

Elaine contributed her interpretation of this saying later during group discussion. After the class had had a chance to think about it, Mr. Kieffer added, "Most of you have been learning through your own experiences, which is certainly one of the best ways. However, writers and thinkers through-out the ages have hoped we might learn through their words. Some of their stories even stem from before words were put down in writing and were shared by storytelling. This is what some people call an oral tradition. Many of these stories are myths."

And he went on, "So, now we're going to start a mythology unit, and we've brought in a lot of books for you to share. After you've had a taste of these, why don't you seek out others of your own."

"And do bring them in to share with the class, please," added Miss Ceprano. "If you notice, we've started a web over there on a chart. It now has a few references for Roman, Greek, Nordic, and Native American myths on it. Please feel free to add to the list any time you and a partner agree on a good reference." Miss Ceprano knew that this would encour-age the sharing of knowledge. "And now, for starters, let's form groups of three, and we'll share some of the literature together through group read-alouds. Please don't forget to stop occasionally for discussion. We'll pass out a group as-sessment sheet later so that you can decide how successfully your group functioned today.

Throughout the week, the students read independently and in pairs or groups. They also brought in many other books, magazine articles, and videos to share. The following week Miss Ceprano invited the entire class to the large-group discussion area and asked, "Now that we've been swimming in myths for a week, what kinds of things come to mind that might be interesting for you to do with one of your favorites?"

Isabella's hand shot into the air. "I know which myth I'd like to crawl into, Miss Ceprano."

Miss Ceprano couldn't disguise the smile that began to tug at the corners of her mouth. She extended daily invitations to her students to "crawl into" this or that piece of text. Funny how much kids learn from us, she thought.

Isabella went on, "I love to read the creation myths. Some of them sound pretty believable and others are pretty weird. I might do something with one of the weird ones, like Cyclops." Mr. Kieffer could well imagine that Isabella would choose a "weird" myth, for she loved drama. He guessed that they might be in for a comedy presentation.

Derinda, who was rapidly becoming a pretty proficient flautist, asked a predictable question: "Can we interpret through music—like we did for *The Ugly Duckling* operetta we wrote?"

"What do you think, class? What kind of rules do you want to put on this project? Todd, would you like to scribe as we make suggestions? Then later we'll revise the list and transfer it to a final draft for reference," suggested Mr. Kieffer.

Together the group developed class guidelines for the project, along with a performance assessment sheet. As the discussion evolved, excitement grew. Finally, Mr. Kieffer suggested that students meet in dyads to brainstorm their intentions. And then he added, "Hand in an outline or web of your plan once you're satisfied with it."

Miss Ceprano tacked some chart paper to the chalkboard. She then modeled her own process plan for the group before each student met with a partner. "I recently read several pieces of literature concerning Gaia. Much of it is related to ecology, which, as most of you know, I have a special interest in. I feel really comfortable with these myths, and I've gone ahead and developed a process plan about how I'm going to proceed. First I'll list the references for my topic. Then I'll write out the story for this myth. Next I'll decide which medium I'd like to use—a play or a song or maybe computer graphics. Last I'll explain how I plan to share my work with others—and maybe it won't just be with our class. How does that sound? Did I leave anything out?" The group had a few questions, for which the others offered possible answers. When everyone seemed comfortable with the project, Miss Ceprano invited them to find a partner and begin brainstorming.

Throughout the project, students deliberated on the direction they would follow for their own presentations. With so much talent in the room, the presentations were sure to be both rich and diverse.

. . . .

IN CONCLUSION

We realize that what we are accomplishing is a drop in the ocean. But if this drop were not in the ocean, it would be missed.

Mother Teresa

This is the kind of text that could go on and on, *ad infinitum*. But there really is no need for that, for *your* own classroom affords a rich abundance of ideas far more relevant than the ones I've offered here. The activities that I have chosen to share are merely stepping stones, prototypes of possibilities. They are not meant to be used as recipes, as were the teacher manuals of yesteryear.

As you reflect on your own classroom community through the book's descriptions of other communities, I hope you and your students will come to create many more meaningful and exciting experiences—ones you and they will remember and use for the rest of your lives.

. . . .

BIBLIOGRAPHY

Student Texts

Andersen, Hans Christian. *The Ugly Duckling*. New York: Scholastic, 1987.

Babbit, Natalie. *Tuck Everlasting*. New York: Farrar, Straus & Giroux, 1975.

Baylor, Byrd. *I'm in Charge of Celebrations*. New York: Scribner's, 1986.

Blume, Judy. *The One in the Middle Is a Green Kangaroo*. New York: Bradbury, 1981.

Blume, Judy. *Tales of a Fourth Grade Nothing*. New York: Dell, 1976.

Burnie, David. *Tree*. New York: Knopf, 1988.

Caudill, Rebecca. *Did You Carry the Flag Today, Charlie?* New York: Holt, Rinehart & Winston, 1966.

Cherry, Lynn. *The Great Kapok Tree*. New York: Harcourt Brace Jovanovich, 1990.

Cowcher, Helen. *Antarctica*. New York: Farrar, Straus & Giroux, 1990.

Cowcher, Helen. *Rainforest*. New York: Farrar, Straus & Giroux, 1988.

Dahl, Roald. *Charlie and the Chocolate Factory*. New York: Puffin, 1964.

Dahl, Roald. *Charlie and the Great Glass Elevator*. New York: Bantam, 1977.

Dahl, Roald. *The Enormous Alligator*. New York: Bantam, 1984.

Dahl, Roald. *James and the Giant Peach*. New York: Bantam, 1981.

D'Aulaire, Ingri & Edgar D'Aulaire. *Greek Myths*. New York: Dell, 1992.

dePaola, Tomie. *Strega Nona*. New York: Prentice Hall, 1975.

Dickens, Charles. *A Christmas Carol*. New York: Scholastic, 1943.

Durell, Ann & Marilyn Sachs (eds.). *The Big Book for Peace*. New York: Dutton, 1990.

Faces. Peterborough, New Hampshire: Cobblestone.

Gag, Wanda. *Millions of Cats*. New York: Putnam, 1977.

Galdone, Paul. *The Little Red Hen*. Boston: Houghton Mifflin, 1985.

Gardiner, John Reynolds. *Stone Fox*. New York: Harper & Row, 1980.

Gates, Frieda & Yoshi Miyake. *Owl Eyes*. New York: Lothrop, Lee & Shepard, 1994.

Gentner, Norma. *Dig a Dinosaur*. Seattle, Washington: The Wright Group, 1993.

Giff, Patricia Reilly. *The Beast in Ms. Rooney's Room*. New York: Dell, 1984.

Giff, Patricia Reilly. *Purple Climbing Days*. New York: Dell, 1985.

Gilford, Henry (adapter). *The Reader's Theater Mythology Plays*. North Billerica, Massachusetts: Curriculum Associates, 1967.

Grimm, Jacob (Brothers Grimm). *Little Red Cap*. New York: Morrow, 1983.

Helprin, Mark. *Swan Lake*. Boston: Houghton Mifflin, 1989.

Hesse, Karen. *Letters from Rifka*. New York: Puffin, 1993.

Hoberman, Mary Ann. *A House Is a House for Me*. New York: Scholastic, 1978.

Hutchins, Pat. *The Doorbell Rang*. New York: Scholastic, 1986.

Kellogg, Steven. *Can I Keep Him?* New York: Dial, 1976.

Macaulay, David. *Motel of Mysteries*. Boston: Houghton Mifflin, 1979.

Melser, June & Joy Cowley. *In a Dark, Dark Wood*. Seattle, Washington: The Wright Group, 1982.

Mitchell, Joni & Alan Baker (ill.). *Both Sides Now*. New York: Scholastic, 1992.

Munsch, Robert. *Moira's Birthday*. Toronto, Ontario: Annick, 1987.

Munsch, Robert. *Mud Puddle*. Toronto, Ontario: Annick, 1986.

Munsch, Robert. *The Paper Bag Princess*. Toronto, Ontario: Annick, 1980.

Munsch, Robert. *Thomas's Snowsuit*. Toronto, Ontario: Annick, 1985.

National Geographic World. Washington, D.C.: National Geographic Society.

Near, Holly. *The Great Peace March*. New York: Holt, Rinehart & Winston, 1986.

O'Dell, Scott. *Island of the Blue Dolphins*. Boston: Houghton Mifflin, 1960.

Paterson, Katherine. *Jacob, Have I Loved*. New York: Avon, 1980.

Paulsen, Gary. *Hatchet*. New York: Macmillan, 1986.

Paulsen, Gary. *Tracker*. New York: Scholastic, 1984.

Raffi. *Down by the Bay*. New York: Crown, 1987.

Raffi. *Like Me and You*. New York: Crown, 1994.

Rainbow. Nairobi, Kenya: Stellagraphics.

Robinson, Barbara. *The Best Christmas Pageant Ever*. New York: Harper & Row, 1972.

Russell, William F. (ed.). *Classic Myths to Read Aloud*. New York: Crown, 1989.

Rylant, Cynthia. *Missing May*. New York: Orchard, 1992.

Seattle, Chief (Susan Jeffers, ill.). *Brother Eagle, Sister Sky*. New York: Scholastic, 1991.

Slobodkina, Esphyr. *Caps for Sale*. New York: Scholastic, 1984.

Smith, Doris. *A Taste of Blackberries*. New York: Scholastic, 1976.

Tapori. Landover, Maryland: Fourth World Movement.

Taylor, Theodore. *The Cay*. New York: Avon, 1969.

Twain, Mark. *The Adventures of Tom Sawyer*. New York: Puffin, 1983.

Van Allsburg, Chris. *Jumanji*. Boston: Houghton Mifflin, 1981.

Van Allsburg, Chris. *The Stranger*. Boston: Houghton Mifflin, 1986.

Young, Ed. *Lon Po Po: A Red Riding Hood Story from China*. New York: Philomel, 1989.

Waber, Bernard. *Ira Sleeps Over*. Boston: Houghton Mifflin, 1972.

Wells, Rosemary. *Noisy Nora*. New York: Dial, 1980.

White, E.B. *Charlotte's Web*. New York: HarperCollins, 1952.

Wilder, Laura Engalls. *Little House in the Big Woods*. New York: Harper & Row, 1932.

Williams, Vera B. & Jennifer Williams. *Stringbean's Trip to the Shining Sea*. New York: Scholastic, 1988.

Wood, Douglas. *Old Turtle*. Duluth, Minnesota: Pfeifer-Hamilton, 1992.

Zeman, Ludmila. *Gilgamesh the King*. Montreal, Quebec: Tundra, 1992.

ZuZu. New York: Restless Youth Press.

Audiotapes

Gentner, Norma. *Dig a Dinosaur*. Seattle, Washington: The Wright Group, 1993.

Mitchell, Joni. *Both Sides Now*. New York: Siquomb Publishing, 1967.

Raffi. *Raffi in Concert with the Rise and Shine Band*. Vancouver, British Columbia: Troubador Records, 1989.

Special Music Company. *Sounds of Nature*. Englewood Cliffs, New Jersey: Essex Entertainment, 1990.

Tropical Jungle. Berkeley, California: Nature Company, 1989.

Professional Sources

Applebee, A.N. *The Child's Concept of Story*. Chicago, Illinois: University of Chicago Press, 1978.

Arlin, M., M. Scott, & J. Webster. "The Effects of Pictures on Rate of Learning Sight Words: A Critique of the Focal Attention Hypothesis." In *Reading Research Quarterly*. Vol. 14, No. 4 (1978-79).

Barr, R. "Studying Classroom Reading Instruction." In *Reading Research Quarterly*. Vol. 21, No. 3 (1986).

Betts, E. *Foundations of Reading Instruction*. New York: American Book Company, 1946.

Bruner, J. *Acts of Meaning*. Cambridge, Massachusetts: Harvard University Press, 1990.

Calkins, L.M. & S. Harwayne. *Living between the Lines*. Portsmouth, New Hampshire: Heinemann, 1991.

Costa, A. & R.J. Garmston. *Cognitive Coaching: A Foundation for Renaissance Schools*. Norwood, Maine: Christopher Gordon, 1994.

Dewey, J. *Democracy and Education*. New York: Macmillan, 1916.

Durkin, D. "What Classroom Observations Reveal about Reading Comprehension Instruction." In *Reading Research Quarterly*. Vol. 14, No. 4 (1978-79).

Eisner, E.W. *The Enlightened Eye: Qualitative Inquiry and the Enhancement of Educational Practice*. New York: Macmillan, 1991.

Garan, E. "Who's in Control? Is There Enough 'Empowerment' to Go Around?" In *Language Arts*. Vol. 71, No. 3 (1994).

Goodman, Y.M., D.J. Watson, & C.L. Burke. *Reading Miscue Inventory*. New York: Richard C. Owen, 1987.

Halliday, M.A.K. *Learning How to Mean: Explorations in the Development of Language*. London: Edward Arnold, 1975.

Harste, J., K. Short, & C. Burke. *Creating Classrooms for Authors*. Portsmouth, New Hampshire: Heinemann, 1988.

Harste, J., V. Woodward, & C. Burke. *Language Stories and Literacy Lessons*. Portsmouth, New Hampshire: Heinemann, 1974.

Heckelman, R.G. "Using the Neurological Impress Remedial Technique." In *Academic Therapy Quarterly*. Vol. 1, No. 3 (1966).

Holdaway, D. *The Foundations of Literacy*. New York: Scholastic, 1987.

Hunt, L. "Six Steps to the Individualized Reading Program (IRP)." In *Elementary English*. Vol. 48, No. 1 (1971).

Illich, I. *Deschooling Society*. New York: Harper & Row, 1970.

Johnson, R. & D. Johnson. "Student-Student Interaction: Ignored but Powerful." In *Journal of Teacher Education*. Vol. 6, No. 4 (1984).

Kibby, M. "The Effects of Certain Instructional Conditions and Response Modes on Initial Word Learning." In *Reading Research Quarterly*. Vol. 15, No. 1 (1979).

Kohn, A. "Caring Kids: The Role of Schools." In *Kappan*. Vol. 72, No. 7 (1991).

Koskinen, P.S. & I.H. Blum. "Paired Repeated Reading: A Classroom Strategy for Developing Fluent Reading." In *The Reading Teacher*. Vol. 40, No. 1 (1986).

Manzo, A. "Guided Reading Procedure." In *Journal of Reading*. Vol. 18, No. 4 (1975).

Noddings, N. *Caring*. Berkeley, California: University of California Press, 1984.

Ogle, D. "K-W-L: A Teaching Model that Develops Active Reading of Expository Text." In *The Reading Teacher*. Vol. 39, No. 6 (1986).

Peck, M.S. *The Different Drum: Community Making and Peace*. New York: Simon & Schuster, 1987.

Rose, L. *Picture This: Teaching through Visualization*. Tucson, Arizona: Zephyr, 1991.

Samuels, S.J. "Automaticity and Repeated Reading." In *Reading Education: Foundations for a Literate America*. J. Osborn, P.T. Wilson, & R.C. Anderson (eds.). Boston, Massachusetts: Lexington, 1979.

Singer, H. "Sight Word Learning with and without Pictures." In *Reading Research Quarterly*. Vol. 15, No. 2 (1980).

Stauffer, R. *Teaching Reading as a Thinking Process*. New York: Harper & Row, 1981.

Topping, K. "Paired Reading: A Powerful Technique for Parent Use." In *The Reading Teacher*. Vol. 42, No. 7 (1989).